D1736421

So Going
Around Cities

The Selected Works Series #4:

Ted
Berrigan

ϕ Blue Wind Press

So Going Around Cities

New & Selected Poems 1958–1979

Berkeley / 1980

The epigraph is excerpted from the poem "Rivers and Mountains" and is © 1977 by John Ashbery. (from *Rivers and Mountains,* Ecco Press, New York, 1977.)

LIBRARY OF CONGRESS CATALOGING IN PUBLICATION DATA:

Berrigan, Ted.
So going around cities. new & selected poems 1958–1979.

(The Selected works series ; 4)
Includes index.
I. Title.

PS3552.E74S57   811'.54   80–10185
isbn 0-912652-62-4
isbn 0-912652-63-2 lim.ed.
isbn 0-912652-61-6 pbk.

This First Edition was designed by George Mattingly, with cover painting (untitled) by Donna Dennis, drawings by George Schneeman, photo of the author by Alain, typeset in Garamond Light and Journal Roman by Dave Mattingly, with mechanicals by Alan Bernheimer, and was manufactured in the United States.

A signed numbered boxed cloth edition of this book is available for $39.95 from Blue Wind Press, Post Office Box 7175, Berkeley, California 94707.

Acknowledgements

• A LILY FOR MY LOVE : Providence, R.I. : Oxford Press : 1959. • THE SON-
NETS : New York City : "C" Press : 1964 : Ron Padgett, Ed. • THE SONNETS :
New York City : Grove Press : 1967 : Donald Allen. • LIVING WITH CHRIS :
New York City : Boke Press : 1965 : Joe Brainard. • BEAN SPASMS : New York
City : Kulchur Press : 1968 : Lita Hornick. • MANY HAPPY RETURNS : New
York City : Corinth Books : 1969 : Ted Wilentz. • DOUBLE–TALK : Iowa City,
Iowa : 1969 : Tom Miller. • IN THE EARLY MORNING RAIN : London, Eng-
land, and New York City : Cape Goliard / Grossman : 1970 : Barry Hall.
• GUILLAUME APOLLINAIRE IST TOT : Cologne, Germany : Marz Verlag :
1970 : Rolf Dieter Brinkmann. • MEMORIAL DAY : New York City : St. Mark's
Poetry Project : 1971 : Anne Waldman, Steve Facey. • MEMORIAL DAY : Lon-
don, England : Aloes Press : 1974 : Allan Fisher, Jim Pennington. • A FEELING
FOR LEAVING : New York City : Frontward Books : 1975 : Rochelle Kraut,
Bob Rosenthal. • RED WAGON : Chicago : Yellow Press : 1976 : Richard
Friedman, Peter Kostakis, Darlene Pearlstein. • NOTHING FOR YOU : Lenox,
Massachusetts : Angel Hair Press : 1977 : Lewis Warsh and Bernadette Mayer.

My thanks to all of the above, & to the editors & publishers of the many maga-
zines, journals, broadsides, & postcards where great numbers of these poems first
appeared.

Special thanks are due to David Gitin, who was in on the beginning of this proj-
ect, and whose initial list of selections for possible inclusion provided me with a
working base from which the final selection of *So Going Around Cities* was built.

Thanks also to the New York State Council for the Arts, which, through the aus-
pices of the American branch of P.E.N., provided me with a grant without which
this book might still be in process; & special thanks to Ms. Christine Friedlander
of P.E.N.

I have always liked the idea of a dedication page, and one follows. At the same
time, it feels appropriate here to record that this book is especially *For:* Joe
Brainard; Dick Gallup; & Ron Padgett.

—Ted Berrigan

Contents

from The Sonnets: NYC 1963

Many Happy Returns: 1961–1968

Not Dying: 1977–1979

Author's Note

The poems are arranged in chronological order, which seemed important to the accuracy of such a book as this, one which might easily have been titled "As Much As Was Possible of The Story So Far." But the individual sections have been allowed to tell their own stories, so calling for some deviation from strict calendar order. The several stories that go to making the one story, *my* story, of necessity overlap, and have been allowed to do so. "My" story in that generally there has been an "I" that, in doing the telling, has by nature located itself in the center of the action, though by no means is *I* always the central character, let alone the hero. My sense, for that matter my ambition, has been to create a character named *I*, in the poems, that, when the actual writing goes on, is speaker, hearer, notater, perceiver, even judge when that is called for.

There are a number of poems scattered throughout the book which have not been published in any other book; so they are also new and selected. The final section is all new poems, as is at least half of the section titled EASTER MONDAY. And, happily, since the final construction of this book, I do have more. Be seeing you.

—Ted Berrigan
Autumn, 1979
New York City

to Alice

to Anselm   *& to Doug*

So going around cities
To get to other places you found
It all on paper but the land
Was made of paper processed
To look like ferns, mud or other
Whose sea unrolled its magic
Distances and then rolled them up
Its secret was only a pocket
After all but some corners are darker
Than these moonless nights spent as on a raft . . .

from Rivers and Mountains
by John Ashbery

So Going
Around Cities

First Poems
1958–1963

"Gus live entirely by hemselve and for hemselve."

POEM

Seven thousand feet over
The American Midwest
In the black and droning night
Sitting awake and alone
I worry the stewardess . . .
Would you like some coffee, sir?
How about a magazine?
No thanks. I smile and refuse.
My father died today. I
Fifteen hundred miles away
Left at once for home, having
received the news from my mother
In tears on the telephone.
He never rode in a plane.

3 PAGES

for Jack Collom

10 Things I do Every Day

play poker
drink beer
smoke pot
jack off
curse

BY THE WATERS OF MANHATTAN

flower

positive & negative

go home

read   lunch   poems

hunker down

changes

Life goes by
quite merrily
blue
NO HELP WANTED

Hunting For The Whale

"and if the weather plays me fair
I'm happy every day."

The white that dries clear
the heart attack
the congressional medal of honor
A house in the country

NOT ENOUGH

\

VALENTINE

I have been here too many times before
you & now it's time to go
crazy again will that make you like me? I think so
often about you & all those bon aperitifs we had
wanted to have but didn't in Paris where we
never got to did we No we didn't although now
Here I am & everyone loves me so
where are you? & why don't they go
away? I didn't ask for this I asked for you
love but you said No, you didn't say
May I? true & crazy here I am
again unkempt in my passion at that May I?

DOUBTS

to David Bearden

Don't call me "Berrigan"
Or "Edmund"
If ever you touch me
Rivers of annoyance undermine the arrangements

If you would own me
Spit
The broken eggshell of morning
A proper application
Of stately rhythms
Timing
Accessible to adepts
All
May pierce this piercing wind
Penetrate this light
To hide my shadow

But the recoil
Not death but to mount the throne
Mountains of twine and
Entangling moments

Which is why I send you my signal

That is why I give you this six-gun and call you "Steve"
Have you taken the measure of the wind?
Can hands touch, and
Must we dispose of "the others"?

PRAYER

Rilke,
I strain to gather my absurdities
Into a symbol. I falter. These
Roisterers here assembled shatter my zest
With festivity.

Once again I turn to you, to your
Buch das Bildung. Oh Tall Tree
In the self
Flower we three into one.
May he who is you
Become me.

NIGHT LETTER

Dear Marge, hello. It is 5:15 a.m.
Outside my room atonal sounds of rain
Drum in the pre-dawn. In my skull my brain
Aches in rhythm to that pounding morning rain.
In your letter, many questions. I read
Them over and over. And now I dread
Answering. "Deteriorating," you said.
Not a question, really, but you did
Say it. And made it hard to write. You know
Margie, tonight, and every night, in any
Season, cold images glitter brightly
In my head. Dreams of Larry Walker
In his marriage bed: of David Bearden
Paranoid: and of Martin Cochran, dead.

POEM

In Joe Brainard's collage its white arrow
does not point to William Carlos Williams.
He is not in it, the hungry dead doctor.
What is in it is sixteen ripped pictures
Of Marilyn Monroe, her white teeth white-
washed by Joe's throbbing hands. "Today
I am truly horribly upset because Marilyn
Monroe died, so I went to a matinee B-movie
and ate King Korn popcorn," he wrote in his
Diary. The black heart beside the fifteen pieces
of glass in Joe Brainard's collage
takes the eyes away from the gray words
Doctor, but they say, "I LOVE YOU"
and the sonnet is not dead.

PEARL HARBOR DAY

Seurat and Juan Gris combine this season
to outline Central Park in geometric
trillion pointed bright red-brown and green-gold
blocks of blooming winter. Trees stand stark-
naked guarding bridal paths like Bowery
Santa Clauses keeping Christmas-safe each city block.
Thus I, red-faced and romping in the wind
Whirl thru mad Manhattan dressed in books
looking for today with tail-pin. I
never place it right, never win. It
doesn't matter, though. The cooling wind keeps blow-
ing and my poems are coming.
Except at night. Then
I walk out in the bleak village and look for you

"DEAR CHRIS

it is 3:17 a.m. in New York city, yes, it is
1962, it is the year of parrot fever. In
Brandenburg, and by the granite gates, the
old come-all-ye's streel into the street. Yes, it is now,
the season of delight. I am writing to you to say that
I have gone mad. Now I am sowing the seeds which shall,
when ripe, master the day, and
portion out the night. Be watching for me when blood
flows down the streets. Pineapples are a sign
that I am coming. My darling, it is nearly time. Dress
the snowman in the Easter sonnet we made for him
when scissors were in style. For now, goodbye, and
all my love,
    The Snake."

HEARTS

At last I'm a real poet I've written a
ballade a sonnet a poem in spontaneous
prose and even a personal poem   I can use
punctuation or not and it doesn't even
matter   I'm obscure when I feel like it
especially in my dream poems which I never even
call   Dream Poem   but from sheer cussedness title
Match Game Etc. (for Dick Gallup) or something like that.

For example, take this poem, I don't know how
to end it, It needs six lines to make it a sonnet, I
could just forget it and play hearts with Joe and
Pat and Dick, but lately I'm always lethargic,
and I don't even like hearts, or Pat, or Joe, or
Dick or/and especially myself, & this is no help.

DECEMBER

Brother and sister departed
With apologies to the mother for intercourse
In their hearts

EPITHALAMION

Pussy put her paw into the pail of paint.
"Hip, hop, pip, pop, tip, top, pop-corn".
The dipper tipped and the sirup dripped upon her apron.
Phillippa put the Parson's parcel beside the Professor's papers.
Bowser buried his bone inside a barrel.
The brown bear stole the bumblebee.
White snow whirled everywhere.
The able laborer objects to the bride.
Adam and Eve stumbled over the rubber tube.
Mama made a muffler and a muff for me.
My Mary's asleep by the murmuring stream
The meadow-mouse uses the lamp for its moonbeam.

In Minneapolis, Minnesota there are many married men.
Many Americans are making money in Mexico.

THE TV STORY

1.

It is after 7 in the evening and raining cold in bed. Next day
12 noon Dick comes by we go to the Museum—with Sandy—
lovely on my naked back through the open window. She has
finished *Nadja*, make entry in my journal, work on my new
poem, go to baby-sitting. Carol came, looking for Dick—kicks
them out. Now I am—I carve a pumpkin. I read *Nadja*. 4 a.m.
—lying naked on the bed. We start talking about Marcel
Duchamp. All try to figure out how pay the rent . . . 12
o'clock . . . ourselves . . . we begin touching one another in
the dark, & she is reading *Prologemena to Greek Religion*.
She says she is—she takes off my clothes & we laugh. Dick & I
discuss Wallace Fowlie, he gives me a copy of *Nadja*, not to
keep—she says if it's ever over between us in your mind
please tell me. Talk about Dada, we do, drink whiskey. He
makes coffee. We let him in, he knocks again—at the door—
we show him a copy of *Nadja*—he dissipates—she interprets
it for him in some new way, I translate it for him, he is
sleeping, Dick comes over, we discuss *Nadja* extensively, next
day 12 noon **we** are all to go To the Museum. (TV Show).

2.

I was charging others to love me, instead
of doing so myself.

3.

The day I see my name in the papers, something
snaps, I'm finished; I sadly enjoy my fame, but
I stop writing.

4.

Now fifty years and nostalgic, I pushed open the door of a cafe and asked for a small beer. At the next table some beautiful young women were talking animatedly and my name is mentioned. "Ah," said one of them, "he may be old, he may be homely, but what difference does that make? I'd give thirty years of my life to become his wife." I looked at her with a proud, sad smile, she smiled back in surprise, I got up, I disappeared.

THE UPPER ARM

for Andy Warhol

Upon this field the physical energies of
Clouds.   He will no longer desire the
Demanding force, an incredible
Fortune has fallen across their paths. I wait
a Payer is paying for the art it releases
Prisoners from the hands
In an automobile accident on the
Face
And achieved enemy face
Paleface changed captive
Photographs later
Were tipped   "What does this mean, my son?"
Became categorical   as in "yes"   held on
The arms and
Powder on a little table
And down in a green forest ravine   near to "her"
Security of the relationship is made utterly
With high stakes and shot at those targets out of
Boughs that spell
"MY PAINTINGS"

PRESENCE

and I am lost in the ringing elevator
he waggles   the fat whiteness of milk
sweeping me to the top
one is reminded of constellations
there there were pine needles
dreams of symbolism
the part that goes over the fence last
star light   the cord "reaches"
it was turkey
sheepish lights   you turned me on
reflecting dilemmas   majorities
Bildungsroman of the bathrobe ride
and the briny sound of the alarm
a funny feeling prompted me out of bed
Love
the top had been "sliced"
ribbons your presence on the white and green sheet
I asked for a Hook-and-Ladder
takes   The End.
in the ideal society pants

Now   we can make some explosions
shine like money
Francis is not a diminutive   thanks
others are less legs
thighs wings breast
Caress the window grease, John
as you are not yet 12
19?   40?   who pulls me down?
that night we slept reverently   (you lust
I must lust in-
vigorating   the sixteen genre

dragon   bottle-opener
spiral cuff-link aerial
facade of the wonderful orient word
"doilies"

Overhead the moon is out
blacking my shoes, face

we were all livid, numinous

Things whip toward the center
licking the palate of his headache
this indicates your future
meditates on his wish which is
hooked onto the top and draped archly

Childhood fuses   a mystery play
Take off your beautiful blouse, you foolish girl!
which ribbons the marvelous laurel   the loop-
Are you list-   with this ring I
eye thee
(that was later, out west, after more baseball
some turkey
a wristwatch, dictionary, sniper suit, rifle
to "meditate"
(is there room in the tune to attune in?)

They were incensed at his arrival
Now we are glad   it was stinky
some paint them black in the face to be quaint or something
one symbol fact seems valid
I don't know
all hate it to be right
on the cards
which are sometimes funky (aesthetic) having
snow of feet and that a domination.
Then we had presence.

MATINEE

Morning
     (ripped out of my mind again!)

AS USUAL

Take off your hat & coat & give me all your money
I have to buy some pills & I'm flat broke

AFTER BREAKFAST

for Brett deBary

You are still there eating ice cream spear in hand on paper
bed chair window heaven two dollars hangs up your life-
jacket gulls tossing and turning out over the day. You don't
sleep ever but get up the bricks have cooled. We stub our toes
on them. Clothes in hand I wait; in the movie out you go
come back with plums a Post one egg: you don't know my
mind. In bed we touch photographs in rainstorms that hold
my breath together don't look at each other lights out China
Night full of V-8 juice and sugar across the room and out the
door mice playing in cans. I think then lay down you giggle
return to consciousness Speech is silver Silence is golden
500 times. A red ball bobs up above the one chair sheds new
light on Hinges In Advance Of The Broken Arm; in this light
everything moves if slightly. You touch a hand mine an alarm
"goes off." Now might I see you your cool shoulder ink stains
your inimitable style smile at your tendered concerns, they
shine, like your eyes, which can't see mine as now I change
in the exact same room 6000 miles away from where we have
remained, awake.

R U S T Y   N A I L S

for Tom Veitch

MY NAME

Smiling with grace the mother, the spouse, leaned
across to the fourth of their after-the-theatre party,
who was a girl older than this boy, aged almost seven-
teen, by perhaps two years.

THE PROBLEM OF EVIL

I led in my childhood and youth the gently-bred existence
of my class and my kind.

PATRIOTISM

An estimated two million wasps were loosed on an area
of four hundred and fifty miles inhabited by
eighty thousand people.

MY BEST FRIEND

That was about you in my story.

AN ORPHAN LEARNS TO COUNT

The Police swooped down in a squad car.

MALNUTRITION

By accident I met some rich homosexuals of the inter-
national queer set who cruise around the world, bumping
into each other in queer joints from New York to Cairo.

CANCER

For there was a heavy curtain over the window, and in the center of the room, an electric light bulb, suspended from the ceiling, was all wrapped in newspaper.

SUNBURN

Loading his gun with one of these buttons, he seated himself on the bed beside his wife, and declared his intention of shooting the witch cat.

DEATH BY DROWNING

For, in respect to the latter branch of the supposition, it should be considered that the most trifling variation of the facts of the two cases might give rise to the most important miscalculations, by diverting thoroughly the two courses of events; very much as, in arithmetic, an error which, in its own individuality, may be inappreciable, produces, at length, by dint of multiplication at all points of the process, a result enormously at variance with the truth.

DEATH IN THE AFTERNOON

She sighed in vain for the chaff and the wheat, not knowing the one from the other.

MASSACRED BY THE INDIANS

Ain' nothin' new about that neither.

BAD NEWS

The man in bed—staring at me appraisingly—was enormous.

SPRING RETURNS

We are drawn to shit because we are imperfect in our uses of the good.

THE PENNILESS WIDOW

He drew his wife's attention to the pustule on the top of my skull for I had removed my hat out of courtesy.

THE DOORS OF PERCEPTION

There were seven to choose from, all putty.

THE TERRORS OF PUBERTY

She didn't realize her belly was more provocative when it had been run through with hatred.

A PROVERB

Meanwhile the papers were reporting masochists shooting tacks, with rubber bands, at apes in zoos.

A MESSAGE FROM THE LOVED ONE

I was horrified.

SYMBOLISM

He must have pressed the wrong button, or several of them, for when the door fretted open he found himself deep underground, with no heart to try again.

THE MODERN CRISIS

"What's this nasty piece of wood stuck in your boobs?"

THE AFTERLIFE

"The Cherry Orchard."

THE WORLD TODAY

"Jungle Law," the man agreed.

DEADLY VISIBLE RAYS

They had many days now when they were very happy.

SOMETHING'S HAPPENING HERE

Your historian will not attempt to list the sights he
pointed out in the multitudinous halls since no one
will ever forget them anyway.

EIGHT SQUARES

A good smell of hot coffee is coming out of the coffee-pot
on the table.

A GIFT

"You in the new winter
                stretch forth your hands"

I AM A MAN OF CONSTANT SORROW

"I know from my own experience that telepathy is a fact."

GUS

for Art Lange

. . . Not far from here he was inside his head there were some sands. Of these 50 gave way to a room, latter resembling manure.

To the right, in a kit, a sort of woman-spanned pond absorbed water cake would form at the bottom keep that in.

The hut rust bin thanks piece of colour.

A little pool gravel made him first step aside. Gus walked up under the arc-light as far as the first person, perceived God. *She* was God, having lance, he took her by the behind and kissed her butt. Gus want fuck, to get the information. He spun off her dress. It was there, and very beautiful, his pecker.

Gus live entirely by hemselve and for hemselve.

He spen days taking off bottles, furnishing room, best system ea heat. For Christ sake! Tryd smoke ham wash.

There was a large cop faggot pursued the secret butterfly near fourteen glass jars tomato and green peas coated the stoppers with quicklime cheese wrapped round with linen strip, then lunged into boiling water: it steamed. He por in difference of temperature, he explode. Only, he were saved.

Then he poured some old sardine, laid veal cutlet inside, and sank the copper. He ball him. He cold. He out again.

He continue the experiment. Shut up. The tin egg chicory lobster fish congratulate hemselve.

Ike Heraclitus, or, "Gus," still elusive, flit on ahead.

Despair defeat labor. The woman fell ill. She laid the copper. It glistens as if about to erupt. At that moment the secret fell in the eye, grace over the golden woman's form.

Then Gus made lunch.

STRING OF PEARLS

Lester Young! why are you playing that clarinet
you know you are Horn in my head? the middle page is
missing god damn it now how will I ever understand Nature
And New Painting? doo doot doo Where is Dick Gallup
his room is horrible it has books in it and paint peeling
a 1934 icebox living on the fifth floor it's
ridiculous

        yes and it's ridiculous to be sitting here
in New York City 28 years old wife sleeping and
Lester playing the wrong sound in 1936 in Kansas City (of
all places) sounding like Benny Goodman (of all people) but
a good sound, not a surprise, a voice, & where was Billie, he
hadn't met her yet, I guess Gallup wasn't born yet neither was
my wife Just me & that icebox I hadn't read HORN by John
Clellon Holmes yet, either

What is rhythm I wonder? Which was George & which Ira
    Gershwin? Why
don't I do more? wanting only to be walking in the New
    York Autumn
warm from coffee I still can feel gurgling under my ribs
climbing the steps of the only major statement in New York City
(Louis Sullivan) thinking the poem I am going to write seeing
the fountains come on wishing I were he

PROBLEMS, PROBLEMS

Joy! you come winging in a hot wind on the breath
of happy sexy music, you are peeping
into my redbloodedness, and I am writing silly lines
like, "I was born, reared, and educated in Tulsa,
Oklahoma," only true of Ron Padgett and not Dan'l Boone or me

Uh-huh a sip of gritty coffee, ripping me out of
my mind, making me feel "funny" is carrying me up-
town past interesting bodegas, the interesting
bums eyeing me, my beard throws them off
tho I'm yearning for a little romance

Dontcha think it's time? thanks & your name is
walking right by my side it hurts me to see you talking
to any other guy! where is Harry Fainlight, he's on a trip
Now that's integrity! Where's Andy Warhol? Far out, but Harry
doesn't think so he prefers Vaughan Traherne Wordsworth even

Who can help but love him? it's so American of him! Lines,
you must be saying what I mean I hope I like you later. Our
Love must be sweet destiny, no other love could thrill me so
completely (unless it be going to the movies, and alone, crossing
the Mississippi for the first time, so rare

a feat for feet "born, reared and educated in Tulsa, Oklahoma"
turned blue with cold and being careful not to touch one another.)

SATURDAY AFTERNOONS ON THE PIAZZA

Why have you billowed under my ancient piazza
Father? "I swan, if you don't beat everything
Anybody ever heard tell of!" Refreshment time!
Have a nonpareil? Thank you! Here we are again

In the movies and I'm holding your thigh, Mmmmmmmmmmm
Feels like "a belly" to me. "Well, I declare, Feety-
Belle, ain't you ever gonna get y'rself a real . . . Shut your face
Angerbelle, you ain't doin' s'hot y'rself y'know,

my stars!" (At intermission I called her at the hotel
And she made a big thing about somebody telling her
"I'm Judy Garland's daughter.") When you're 7 or 8 or 9
You don't really care who your momma and poppa are,

Just so they really love you and have TV and all that.
Up in the blue window a white woman is reeling out her laundry.

TRUTH AS HISTORY

1.

My rooms were full of awful features when
I was burning, dear, and you were eating goblets
of ruinous dinner! It didn't matter, tho. The
foolish wind kept blowing, and my bones were hum-
ming! That was when my eyes walked out
on to bleak piers and shrieked for you! You were standing, often,
stark-naked just as if you knew it wasn't raining
and no-one had stolen all the dazzling looks. But this
one time the saboteurs sneaked up! Hah! I didn't
let them grind you, my little Coolie-Baby, who insures
my factory. No, and it's not bad to lay buried, in Hoovers-
ville, by wires, laid on us by gentlemen, & ladies flushed
with gin. Except at night, when you are lying in the wind.

2.

I beat on the fruits of the gushy showers
burning up ginger-ale, only a pantomime mother &
father, doting on feelable widows, as my rent & these
urgent denials in my plug-ugly vision hold out! I
would take some corn to Minton's & throw it on Dizzy
Gillespie, & I mumble at babies on the bus, although
I too am reading the nickel journals, while my axles
are losing patience. Castles! my dearest, the whole town
is hiding out in six cheap hotels, sorrowful you gaping at me
as I continue to concoct ewe dreams! I would like very much
to be in your hair, in hottest blood, my Saxon Thing was nursed
on Western fiction with Doc Holliday my Christopher
Columbus to help me. But it's no use, you love Oliver Hardy, he's
the last of the old-time newsboys. I have a soggy bed.

IKONOSTASIS

for Bernadette Mayer

Kings   . . . panties
I imagine these here
the difference between past and dreaming
An uncomfortable Dodge
The word dissolves
iron things
Horses for example
then there is the other which may be called
the familiar floating oasis
larger than whiter
brazen, resourceful
. . . sinning palms balance it

perhaps these are wax detectors
and create situations
a magic shell for silliness
before the law tables
of this here
Heart
That has been tinted white
by way of exercise

the Political
glazes
These eyes
breaks
into the grocery store where
is sick   cannot work

twisted stick

industrial berry shoes are established
above all   . . . be double
                        or collapse

the wall covered with glass character weather

M'sieur Negro-at-3 A.M.
Charioteer
His burning problem

it doesn't stop the music
the magic
under tasteless stockings
and under the sting which leaves no ash

the grey snow of someone's epoch annoys
and redeems
through certain fraudulent practices which,
like sulphur, blacken

making an undenied hash of all that
and that will now not melt in the first sunbeam
being its own muse

AUTUMN'S DAY

after Rilke

Lord, it is time. Summer was very great.
Now cast your shadow upon sundials.
Let winds remind meadows it is late.

Mellow now the last fruits on the vine.
Allow them only two more southern days.
Hasten them to fulness, and press
The last heavy sweetness through the wine.

Who has no home can not build now.
Who dwells alone must now remain alone;
Will waken, read, write long letters, and
Will wander restlessly when leaves are blowing.

from The Sonnets
NYC, 1963

"It is a human universe."
— Charles Olson

Stronger than alcohol, more great than song,
deep in whose reeds great elephants decay;
I, an island, sail, and my shores toss
on a fragrant evening, fraught with sadness
bristling hate.
It's true, I weep too much. Dawns break
slow kisses on the eyelids of the sea,
what other men sometimes have thought they've seen.
And since then I've been bathing in the poem
lifting her shadowy flowers up for me,
and hurled by hurricanes to a birdless place
the waving flags, nor pass by prison ships
O let me burst, and I be lost at sea!
and I fall on my knees then, womanly.

POEM IN THE TRADITIONAL MANNER

Whenever Richard Gallup is dissevered,
Fathers and teachers, and dæmons down under the sea,
Audenesque Epithalamiums! She
Sends her driver home and she stays with me.

Match-Game etcetera! Bootleggers
Barrel-assing chevrolets grow bold. I summon
To myself sad silent thoughts,
Opulent, sinister, and cold.

Shall it be male or female in the tub?
And grawk go under, and grackle disappear,
And high upon the Brooklyn Bridge alone,
An ugly ogre masturbates by ear:

Of my darling, my darling, my pipe and my slippers,
Something there is is benzedrine in bed:
And so, so Asiatic, Richard Gallup
Goes home, and gets his gat, and plugs his dad.

FROM A SECRET JOURNAL

My babies parade waving their innocent flags
an unpublished philosopher, a man who *must*
column after column down colonnade of rust
in my paintings, for they are present
I am wary of the mulctings of the pink promenade,
went in the other direction to Tulsa,
glistering, bristling, cozening whatever disguises
S of Christmas John Wayne will clown with
Dreams, aspirations of presence! Innocence gleaned,
annealed! The world in its mysteries are explained,
and the struggles of babies congeal. A hard core is formed.
"I wanted to be a cowboy." Doughboy will do.
Romance of it all was overwhelming
daylight of itself dissolving and of course it rained.

REAL LIFE

1. *THE FOOL*

He eats of the fruits of the great Speckle
Bird, pissing in the grass! Is it possible
He is incomplete, bringing you Ginger Ale
Of the interminably frolicsome gushing summer showers?
You were a Campfire Girl,
Only a part-time mother and father; I
Was large, stern, acrid, and undissuadable!
Ah, Bernie, we wear complete
The indexed Webster Unabridged Dictionary.
And lunch is not lacking, ants and clover
On the grass. To think of you alone
Suffering the poem of these states!
Oh Lord, it is bosky, giggling happy here,
And you, and me, the juice at last extinct!

2. *THE FIEND*

Red-faced and romping in the wind
I too am reading the technical journals, but
Keeping Christmas-safe each city block
With tail-pin. My angels are losing patience,
Never win. Except at night. Then
I would like a silken thread
Tied round the solid blooming winter.
Trees stand stark-naked guarding bridal paths;
The cooling wind keeps blowing, and
There is a faint chance in geometric boxes!
It doesn't matter, though, to show he is
Your champion. Days are nursed on science fiction
And you tremble at the books upon the earth
As my strength and I walk out and look for you.

PENN STATION

On the green a white boy goes
And he walks. Three ciphers and a faint fakir
No   One   Two   Three   Four   Today
I thought about all those radio waves
Winds flip down the dark path of breath
Passage   the treasure   Gomangani   I
Forget   bring the green boy white ways
And the wind goes there
Keats was a baiter of bears
Who died of lust   (You lie! You lie!)
As so we all must in the green jungle
Under a sky of burnt umber we bumble to
The mien florist's to buy green nosegays
For the fey Saint's parade   Today
We may read about all those radio waves

XIII

Mountains of twine and
Teeth braced against it
Before gray walls. Feet walk
Released by night (which is not to imply
Death) under the murk spell
Racing down the blue lugubrious rainway
To the big promise of emptiness
In air we get our feet wet . . . . a big rock
Caresses cloud bellies
He finds he cannot fake
Wed to wakefulness, night which is not death
Fuscous with murderous dampness
But helpless, as blue roses are helpless.
Rivers of annoyance undermine the arrangements.

XXIII

On the 15th day of November in the year of the motorcar
Between Oologah and Pawnee
A hand is writing these lines
In a roomful of smoky man names burnished dull black
Southwest, lost doubloons rest, no comforts drift
On dream smoke down the sooted fog ravine
In a terrible Ozark storm the Tundra vine
Blood ran like muddy inspiration: Walks he in around anyway
The slight film has gone to gray-green children
And seeming wide night. Now night
Is a big drink of waterbugs   Then were we so fragile
Honey scorched our lips
On the 15th day of November in the year of the motorcar
Between Oologah and Pawnee

XXVII

Andy Butt was drunk in the Parthenon
Bar. If only the Greeks were a band-
Aid, he thought. Then my woe would not flow
O'er the land. He considered his honeydew
Hand. "O woe, woe!" said Andrew, "a fruit
In my hand may suffice to convey me to Greece,
But I must have envy to live! A grasshopper,
George, if you please!" The bartender sees
That our Andrew's awash on the sofa
Of wide melancholy. His wound he refurbishes
Stealthily shifty-eyed over the runes. "Your
Trolleycar, sir," 's said to Andy, "you bloody
Well emptied the Parthenon!" "A fruitful vista
This Our South," laughs Andrew to his Pa,
But his rough woe slithers o'er the Land.

XXXI

And then one morning to waken perfect-faced
To the big promise of emptiness
In a terrible Ozark storm
Pleasing John Greenleaf Whittier!
Speckled marble bangs against his soiled green feet
And each sleeping son is broke-backed and dumb
In fever and sleep processional
Voyages harass the graver
And grope underneath the most serious labor
Darius feared the boats. Meanwhile
John Greenleaf Whittier was writing. Meanwhile
Grandma thought wistfully of international sock fame
Down the John G. Whittier Railroad Road
In the morning sea mouth

XXXVII

It is night. You are asleep. And beautiful tears
Have blossomed in my eyes. Guillaume Apollinaire is dead.
The big green day today is singing to itself
A vast orange library of dreams, dreams
Dressed in newspaper, wan as pale thighs
Making vast apple strides towards "The Poems."
"The Poems" is not a dream. It is night. You
Are asleep. Vast orange libraries of dreams
Stir inside "The Poems." On the dirt-covered ground
Crystal tears drench the ground. Vast orange dreams
Are unclenched. It is night. Songs have blossomed
In the pale crystal library of tears. You
Are asleep. A lovely light is singing to itself,
In "The Poems," in my eyes, in the line, "Guillaume
    Apollinaire is dead."

XXXVIII

Sleep half sleep half silence and with reasons
For you I starred in the movie
Made on the site
Of Benedict Arnold's triumph, Ticonderoga, and
I shall increase from this
As I am a cowboy and you imaginary
Ripeness begins corrupting every tree
Each strong morning   A man signs a shovel
And so he digs   It hurts   and so
We get our feet wet in air   we love our lineage
Ourselves   Music, salve, pills, kleenex, lunch
And the promise never to truckle   A man
Breaks his arm and so he sleeps   he digs
In sleep half silence and with reason

L I I

for Richard White

It is a human universe: & I
is a correspondent   The innocence of childhood
is not genuine   it shines forth from the faces
The poem upon the page is as massive as Anne's thighs
Belly to hot belly we have laid

                       baffling combustions
are everywhere   graying the faces of virgins
aching to be fucked   we fondle their snatches
and O, I am afraid!   The poem upon the page
will not kneel   for everything comes to it
gratuitously   like Gertrude Stein to Radcliffe
Gus Cannon to say "I called myself Banjo Joe!"
O wet kisses, death on earth, lovely fucking in the poem
    upon the page,
you have kept up with the times, and I am glad!

LIII

The poem upon the page is as massive as
Anne's thighs   belly to hot belly we have laid
Serene beneath feverous folds, flashed cool
in our white heat   hungered   and tasted   and
Gone to the movies   baffling combustions
are everywhere!   like Gertrude Stein at Radcliffe,
Patsy Padgett replete with teen-age belly!   every-
one's suddenly pregnant and no one is glad!
O wet kisses, the poem upon the page
Can tell you about teeth you've never dreamed
Could bite, nor be such reassurance! Babies are not
Like Word Origins and cribbage boards   or dreams
of correspondence!   Fucking is so very lovely
Who can say no to it later?

L V

Grace to be born and live as variously as possible
White boats   green banks   black dust   atremble
Massive as Anne's thighs upon the page
I rage in a blue shirt at a brown desk in a
Bright room sustained by a bellyful of pills
"The Poems" is not a dream   for all things come to them
Gratuitously   In quick New York we imagine the blue Charles
Patsy awakens in heat and ready to squabble
No Poems she demands in a blanket command   belly
To hot belly we have laid   serenely white
Only my sweating pores are true in the empty night
Baffling combustions are everywhere! we hunger and taste
And go to the movies   then run home drenched in flame
To the grace of the make-believe bed

L X X

after Arthur Rimbaud

Sweeter than sour apples flesh to boys
The brine of brackish water pierced my hulk
Cleansing me of rot-gut wine and puke
Sweeping away my anchor in its swell
And since then I've been bathing in the poem
Of the star-steeped milky flowing mystic sea
Devouring great sweeps of azure green and
Watching flotsam, dead men, float by me
Where, dyeing all the blue, the maddened flames
And stately rhythms of the sun, stronger
Than alcohol, more great than song,
Fermented the bright red bitterness of love
I've seen skies split with light, and night,
And surfs, currents, waterspouts; I know
What evening means, and doves, and I have seen
What other men sometimes have thought they've seen

L X X I I

for Dick Gallup

The logic of grammar is not genuine   it shines forth
From The Boats   We fondle the snatches of virgins
          aching to be fucked
And O, I am afraid!   Our love has red in it   and
I become finicky as in an abstraction!
                                        (. . . but lately
I'm always lethargic . . .   the last heavy sweetness
through the wine . . .)
                         Who dwells alone
                         Except at night
(. . . basted the shackles the temporal music the spit)
     Southwest lost doubloons rest, no comforts drift on
dream smoke
                    (my dream   the big earth)
On the green a white boy goes   to not
Forget   Released by night (which is not to imply
Clarity   The logic is not The Boats   and O, I am not alone

LXXIV

"The academy of the future
is opening its doors"
—*John Ashbery*

The academy of the future is opening its doors
my dream a crumpled horn
Under the blue sky the big earth is floating into "The Poems."
"A fruitful vista, this, our South," laughs Andrew to his Pa.
But his rough woe slithers o'er the land.
Ford Madox Ford is not a dream. The farm
was the family farm. On the real farm
I understood "The Poems."
          Red-faced and romping in the wind, I, too,
am reading the technical journals. The only travelled sea
that I still dream of
is a cold, black pond, where once
on a fragrant evening fraught with sadness
I launched a boat frail as a butterfly

Many Happy Returns
1961–1968

"so why
are my hands shaking I should know better"

WORDS FOR LOVE

for Sandy

Winter crisp and the brittleness of snow
as like make me tired as not. I go my
myriad ways blundering, bombastic, dragged
by a self that can never be still, pushed
by my surging blood, my reasoning mind.

I am in love with poetry. Every way I turn
this, my weakness, smites me. A glass
of chocolate milk, head of lettuce, dark-
ness of clouds at one o'clock obsess me.
I weep for all of these or laugh.

By day I sleep, an obscurantist, lost
in dreams of lists, compiled by my self
for reassurance. Jackson Pollock   René
Rilke   Benedict Arnold   I watch
my psyche, smile, dream wet dreams, and sigh.

At night, awake, high on poems, or pills
or simple awe that loveliness exists, my lists
flow differently. Of words bright red
and black, and blue.   Bosky.   Oubliette.   Dis-
severed. And O, alas

Time disturbs me. Always minute detail
fills me up. It is 12:10 in New York. In Houston
it is 2 p.m. It is time to steal books. It's
time to go mad. It is the day of the apocalypse
the year of parrot fever! What am I saying?

Only this. My poems do contain
wilde beestes. I write for my Lady
of the Lake. My god is immense, and lonely
but uncowed. I trust my sanity, and I am proud. If
I sometimes grow weary, and seem still, nevertheless

my heart still loves, will break.

PERSONAL POEM #2

I wake up 11:30 back aching from soft bed Pat
gone to work Ron to class (I never heard a sound)
it's my birthday. 27. I put on birthday
pants birthday shirt go to ADAM's buy a Pepsi for
breakfast come home drink it take a pill
I'm high!
       I do three Greek lessons to make
up for cutting class. I read birthday book
(from Joe) on Juan Gris real name: José
Vittoriano Gonzalez stop in the middle read
all my poems gloat a little over new ballad
quickly skip old sonnets imitations of Shakespeare.
Back to books. I read poems by Auden Spenser Stevens
Pound and Frank O'Hara. I hate books.
                    I wonder
if Jan or Helen or Babe ever think about me. I
wonder if David Bearden still dislikes me. I wonder
if people talk about me secretly. I wonder if
I'm too old. I wonder if I'm fooling myself
about pills. I wonder what's in the icebox.
I wonder if Ron or Pat bought any toilet paper
                        this morning

PERSONAL POEM #7

for John Stanton

It is 7:53 Friday morning in the Universe
New York City to be somewhat exact
I'm in my room wife gone working Gallup
fucking in the room below

               had 17½ milligrams desoxyn
last night 1 Miltown, read Paterson, parts
1 & 2, poems by Wallace Stevens & How Much Longer
Shall I Be Able To Inhabit The Divine Sepulchre
(John Ashbery). Made lists of lines to
steal, words to look up (didn't). Had steak & eggs
with Dick while Sandy sweetly slept.

At 6:30 woke Sandy
fucked til 7 now she's late to work & I'm still
high. Guess I'll write to Bernie today
and Tom. And call Tony. And go out at 9 (with Dick)
to steal books to sell, so we can go
to see A NIGHT AT THE OPERA

PERSONAL POEM #8

It's 5:03 a.m. on the 11th of July this morning
and the day is bright gray turning green   I can't stop
loving you says Ray Charles   and I know exactly
what he means because the Swedish policeman in the
next room is beating on my door demanding sleep
and not Ray Charles and bluegrass   does he know
that in three hours I go to court to see if the world
will let me have a wife   he doesn't of course it wouldn't
occur to him   nor would it occur to him to write
"scotch-tape body" in a notebook but it did occur to
John Stanton alias The Knife Fighter age 18 so why
are my hands shaking I should know better

PERSONAL POEM #9

It's 8:54 a.m. in Brooklyn it's the 26th of July
and it's probably 8:54 in Manhattan but I'm
in Brooklyn   I'm eating English muffins and drinking
Pepsi and I'm thinking of how Brooklyn is New
York City too   how odd   I usually think of it
as something all its own   like Bellows Falls   like
Little Chute   like Uijongbu
                       I never thought
on the Williamsburg Bridge I'd come so much to Brooklyn
just to see lawyers and cops who don't even carry guns
taking my wife away and bringing her back
                            No
and I never thought Dick would be back at Gude's
beard shaved off long hair cut and Carol reading
his books when we were playing cribbage and watching
the sun come up over the Navy Yard a-
cross the river
                  I think I was thinking
when I was ahead I'd be somewhere like Perry street
erudite dazzling slim and badly-loved
contemplating my new book of poetry
to be printed in simple type on old brown paper
feminine marvelous and tough

FOR YOU

for James Schuyler

New York's lovely weather hurts my forehead
here where clean snow is sitting, wetly
round my ears, as hand-in-glove and
head-to-head with Joe, I go reeling
up First Avenue to Klein's. Christmas
is sexy there. We feel soft sweaters
and plump rumpled skirts we'd like to try.
It was gloomy being broke today, and baffled
in love: Love, why do you always take my heart away?
But then the soft snow came sweetly falling down
and head in the clouds, feet soaked in mush
I rushed hatless into the white and shining air,
glad to find release in heaven's care.

A PERSONAL MEMOIR
OF TULSA, OKLAHOMA / 1955-60

There we were, on fire with being there, then
And so we put our pants on
And began to get undressed. You were there, then
And there where you were, we were. And I
Was there, too! We had no pants on.

And I saw your penis there. It was right there, where
We were, and it was with us. We looked at it, there
And you said, "Why hello there, Oliver!" to me, there
Beside you, without any pants on, there where I
Could hear you saying, "Why hello there!"

Then Frank came in, and George, and Bill, and Cannonball,
    and Frank;
And Simon, Jonas, Jennie-Lou, and Bob; and gentle Millie-Jean;
And Hannibal the Alp; and they took off their hats and coats
And all began to puke. They puked on Cal, and on Billy, and
On Benjamin, Lucifer, Jezebel, Asthmador and Frank. Then they left.

Frank was much younger then, there, and he had hair
On his belly; he looked like a model-aeroplane; a dark, gloomy
Navel in its tail; and you were there, there
In his tail; you were there and
Hair was there, and air was there, there, up in the air, among
The hair. And you were saying, "Why, hello there!"

And your pants, when you finally put them on there
Had a hole in them, there, where your penis was, before it flew
Away from there to find itself. And the hole there was wide
And it was deep. It was dark there; and
Supersonic Aeroplanes were there. And they were whirring.

"Whirr-whirr-whirr," went the throbbing aeroplanes, as
They zoomed out at us from in there; for we were there, where
Your pants met the sea, and we were glad! I was there, and Jock
And Zack, and Brett; and we met your penis passing by. It said,
"Goodbye mild starlight of The Sign of Fawn," as it rode
                    into the galaxy named 'Fangs.'

TAMBOURINE LIFE

for Anne Kepler

1

FUCK COMMUNISM

it's red white and blue

in the bathroom

(Tuli's)

One dollar, you Mother!

Make all your friends

STOP!

(now there's an idea)

ARTFORUM
723½ La Cienega Blvd
Los Angeles, California

Back to the wall

(it's all in California)

Thanks to Jack

I mean it's all right here
    it's morning
    and I'm looking   over the wall
    at Mr. Pierre Loti   and his nameless dog
    they work well   together
    on paper   i.e. this here

chasing a tiger across white expansiveness
        that is not lacking in significance

(what is?)

THE RUSSIAN REVOLUTION
circa 1967

2

The apples are red again in Chandler's valley
redder for what happened there

                      never did know what it was
never did care

          The End
          on a pillow
              naturally
  a doormat   lust   steam   a hiss   Guilty!

          I see some handwriting on the wall

            of the Williamsburg Bridge

                intersection

          New York Post   ten cents

    tip the newsboy
          over
            a million
             laughs
       that's the party line

                 yes

     he's working on the paper:

            Mr. Horatio Alger

(he has a lovely talent)

thank you

here's your change

3

I'm touched
here, take this penny
there is no need for the past
the sun is out
it's night
I mean
it is night
and I love you better
since
this seizure   of my eyeballs

•

Take off those Fug panties!
Go ahead
it's a big world
The big guys do it

TO ANNIE
(between Oologah & Pawnee)
Guillaume Apollinaire

4

The bodies of my days
open up
in the garden
of
my memory,
America

•

        I have had the courage to look backward
it was like polio
      I shot my mouth off

•

    I NEED MONEY
    that money
    that at least
    at last
    means less
    than a Band-aid
    or a toadstool

•

    OUCH!

    that Band-aid has an OUCH! in it

Who notices a toadstool in the street?
                       Everyone
        who has on
        a Band-aid
                That toadstool has a Band-aid on it

                 5

"He doesn't know how to take a vacation"
                      Dick
     doesn't know how to take a vacation
                     either

        That is not to infer
        that Dick is a toad
        under his Band-aid
                far from it

a toad is a cold-blooded fellow
Dick is warm and full of blood

> When you leave, Dick
> turn the refrigerator
> to vacation please

6

Now I'm going to read 3 cereal poems:
> CORN FLAKES
> OATMEAL
> RY-KRISP
>> thank you
>> they were composed
> excuse me
I mean NOT composed
>> using the John-Cage-Animal-Cracker

> Method of Composition
> (this seems to be mushrooming into a
> major work
> of high
>> seriousness)

•

> I'd fight for that!

(I didn't have to.)

7

True Love

> there is only one way
> to describe
>> "True Love"

does anyone know
that one way?

•

Mr. Nelson Algren
1958 West Evergreen
Chicago, Illinois

•

In Chicago, Illinois, you
are really at home
whether you like it or not, baby,

&, whether you like it
or not

You Are My Friend

so don't pees me off!

8

Come into my house
tonight
Dick
and I will show you
this new work
"House at Night"
It & this page, there not here, are not the same
except in a
'manner of
speaking'

it is not
"A Portrait of Jean-Marie"
tho it cd be

it is also not
"A Portrait of Barbara Harris"
whom I don't know
though I like her plenty

she's a lot like me
(my own name is
"Mr. Brigadoon")

9

I am constantly being caught up
in my own commotion
it is now a slow commotion

The radio is turning me on

10

Commotion over, clothes in hand I wait
in Mr. Ron Padgett's furlined
bridge-jacket

who shivers now
in Paris, Oklahoma
between Galveston &
Mobile a word
incidentally
invented
cross that out
coined
by Mr. Marcel Duchamp

to describe a
lady finger

11

it's too cold in here / but not for me
in my present balloon state / to write this love song

"Cold rosy dawn in New York City"

hovering over the radio
de-dum

12

I woke up this morning
it was night
you were on my mind   LADY BRETT
looking for a home
for the boll weevil

nothing like that in New York City
it's all in Oklahoma
where you-all
can learn to talk like me

if "you-all" is Mr.
Ron Padgett, "The
American Express"

13

He's a good friend of mine
although   he fears he is unable to love
            people
      who have politesse
            whatever that may be
thanks anyway, Frank
you're not without *con brio*
n'es ca'fe?

(thanks, Ed)

14

I quote
from "The Code of the West"

a work
by Mr. Ed Sanders

whose "Poem From Jail"
I highly recommend

On second thought
I quote instead

This work
by Mr. Marcel Duchamp

which
oddly enough

I also give high recommendation

15

THE CODE OF THE WEST

1. Sob when you read "Black Beauty."
2. The true test of a man is a bunt.
3. Dare to do your duty.
4. Press the tip of the tongue on the gums
   behind the upper teeth as for t, and expel
   the breath with vibrations of the vocal cords.
5. He went to the windows of those who slept
   and over each pain like a fairy wept.
6. Halt!
7. Loosen your snood.
8. Close your eyes and doze.

9. Jove! Jove! This shepherd's passion
   is much upon my fashion!
10. Drill.

16

you know
once people paid no attention to me

Mayakovsky

in the garden of my memory

& now
    passion's flower

            wilts
            constantly
            because
                    my lady love is a Holy Roller!

                her body is a sponge
                it has no mud

        Tonight's heat
        will dry that mud
        and it will fall into dust

                            I'm ready for it

                            the body I mean
                            not the dust

            however if you are in the dust
                    kindly hop into this tub of black water please

now hand me that quail
lean me against the belly of a woman
                            (you are that woman)

knock on the door of her house
                 knock-knock
the sun is out
river flowing in a window
a geranium trembling automobile
droning
across the screen
                     Turn back to look
           you don't see
           the door open
           you are standing there
                                 I mean
                                 I am sitting here
                  between the door
                  to a world full of others
                       like yourselves
and the droning solitude of this here Los Angeles
                  Freeway

                  •

            How to get off?

               18

            Hi, Bears!

do you believe in magic?

          good!

          because I am here
          to make a monkey out of you
The best way
to make yrself a monkey
is to jump down

(spin around)
pick a bale of cotton

                if you don't understand
                that
                you will never understand
                your country's history

        1000 volumes a year
        ooze from the minds
            of dead monkeys
          and yet
        we are still too dull
          to understand
            them
                or that

KISS ME!   it is not at all unpleasant
          to be kissed by a monkey
       if you are a monkey
              I am not a monkey
          I do not have a monkey on my back

       I am not a monkey's uncle

       turn page

            19

Only a monkey would read this

       THE ENCYCLOPEDIA OF FLIES
          over 250 flies
      photographed
    in living color

These 250 flies were tied "up"
    executed
by hand
      Not my hand

The Little Sisters

20

There are no flies on me, New York City

21

There are, however,
    two sorts of landscapes here

      the interior
      and
      the exterior

  as well as the other
    which we will not go into here

22

One song I have always liked
    is
      "Hope you Happy Monkey"

  that's the truth

  by Ruth Krauss

23

There you are
There I go
          past The Majestic Men's Clothes
            slightly disheveled
     is a nice phrase
              it has impact
              like the three pricks
                 Alice gave
                Joe Gould
            in 1933
                 MOTHER
              that's Alice's idea of Wonderland

24

She happens to be a sex expert, among other things
if you are squeamish I'd better not tell you
WHAT other things . . .
            "How did Red China get the 'O' bomb?"
                no one knows
              No one will ever know

because no one
     is a tautology

            let's have no truck
                with tautologies

25

         This poem
           has no truck

although it does provide
a sort of Reader's Digest
of Oriental sex practices

                    under the sheets

               Who threw the panties into
                               Mother's tea
             is a good example of one
             of the many unanswered questions
                                    life provides

Where did the beautiful
British secret agent
                    lose his nightie
                        is another

                it was not a majestic nightie
             nor was it a man's nightie
                        unless of course
                        the Beautiful British
                        secret agent
              was a female impersonator
Perhaps that was his secret
            There has always been a
              quick turnover
        among British secret agents
          Look!   there goes one now

26

I am here today   a gentleman
    with time on my hands
        you are in my heart

                        during
                    The Four Seasons
        which are
                        1. springtime

                        2. bedtime

                    and so on

                            27

            There is a revolution going on in my skin
I have the gift of young skin
                                    no pimples
                which is why I am here today

I would like to introduce myself

                        However
                            it will be better
                        between us
    if I don't   cheat

            The victory is not always to the sweet

so keep on the ball, buddy, i.e.
                I mean "the button"

                            28

                    COME ALIVE
                    Meet Me At The Smoke Ring
            Get Your Piles Out of Vietnam
            Let's Love One Another
                        Equality for Homosexuals
                YES
                            SUCK

Stand Up For Dikes

Commemorating The Visit
of Pope Paul X
to NYC
1965

We Won't Go

I'm for Legalized
Abortion

NO MAN IS GOOD THREE TIMES

29

Life certainly is marvelous
When you're in love
                isn't it?

                        Consequently, it is important
                              to be in love
                        most all the time
                        but not all of the time

When you are in love
all of the time
                you get bored   because
                                    life
                when it's always the same
                                        is boring
        isn't it?
                that's a strange theory

30

                it's a theory of strange

        I am in love
        right now. I am in love with
                        (fill in name of person in room)

see me about this later, (

I am not in love with Mr. Walter Steck

        He was or
        was not
            recently elected
     to the assembly
Just for the record   I found Mr. Walter Steck
           recently

               at five o'clock in the afternoon
               on Garcia Lorca's birthday
            lying in the gutter
                  on his button   *shame*

           31

        O ship of states
       Sail on, O allegorical poem

           32

Branching out
shooting all night
he grounded
himself

on the button

           33

      so here
          you stand
    hitting upon things
    you hadn't thought upon

                        when you get into the pictures
                             you wake up
                             inside an oval
                                portrait
                           I mean a woman
              A beautiful reminder sitting on a line

      It could be a steamship line   or even a ferry line

                                34

Life is Never boring when you are Tarzan of the Apes
       e.g.   You step out from behind a bush
                       and you say
                       "Yes, I am M'sieur Tarzan"

                                35

Dick Gallup arrives at this point
and says
                   "Life is Boring"

                                36

Jacques-Louis David is crying in his crib
              he is not bored
                        Jane has given him a banana

                                37

Dick reads those lines
they bore him

                        but I laugh plenty

38

David is sobbing bitterly
in the jungle

"Shut up
or I'll kill you," etc.

He doesn't want to

39

He wants the white
tempera
paint

with which I am painting out the words
in this here comic book

Tarzan of the Apes

so that I can "fill in the words"

40

"The Words" is a good book
It is the autobiography of Mr. Jean-Paul Sartre
from age zero to ten

In it
he tells what a little shit he was.

"I'm going doo-doo" says Jacques-Louis David
we have words
and he falls into sleep

41

Life is long

it's sure been a long Times
crossword puzzle

since I last
was here

That Spring of '65
that was

That was my best year

that was also a good year for

Dancers
Buildings and
People in the Street

in the cell block
a boy
invented

the mahogany cage
before he rested

The climate became a song

Crowds disperse my
purpose
my great calm

Dim lights
turn me down

the radio parts
the curly hair
me on the floor

saying

42

"Go now
        and get me a vast Band-aid"

43

I'm sitting here thinking that these words that I have been
    borrowing from Mr. James "The Rock" Proust & Sons
          should stretch to the end of at least one
                  period in my life.

                        They did.

44

"What I really like is new girls to fuck."

            that's a good line

                          it was said by Dick Gallup
                    who let it drop there
                        that to be explained later

        in the backroom
            of The Peace Eye
                    that's all I know

45

Cow a is not Cow b
    Dick

                        Count Korzybski said that
                that Polish cocksucker
            is what a drunk called HIM
                        He didn't mean Korzybski

                              though
                      He'd never heard of Him
                 I don't know what he meant
                          I was drunk
                   He was speaking Polish
                             He didn't dig Counts
That's a fact

                    46

According to FACT
                    William Burroughs
                           studied under
                           that Polish cocksucker
                                    in Chicago

I've always admired Count Korzybski
and, in fact, I've always admired William Burroughs
                                    Hi Bill!
              I do not, however, admire FACT Magazine
          because it costs too much money
                    and probably for other reasons
                    too vague to be present

                    47

                 dot dot dot

                    48

Listen:

                    Is there a *Pseudotsuga Menziesii*
                       in your house?

        if so, there is
        nothing to worry about

it would be hard to find
a house
in America
where *Pseudotsuga Menziesii* isn't
all over the goddam place

        it has a lovely talent

49

cross something out here

50

        Imagine yourself
        driving on a super highway
        with your friend
            Mr. Bob Harris

besides being a genius
he is also a perennial
problem child
        who mooches off his friends
        sleeps with any available women
        ignores his children
        and smokes ceaselessly
            like yourself

        you may have to stop often
        to relieve yourself
        because your friend
        suffers
        from a terrible disease previously unmentioned
        but not in this poem
            nor by anyone whom you have ever known
        in this vale of tears

back on the freeway   the cars pass
      over your eyes ears nose and throat   and hairs
      no interviews   no photographs
      no autographs
         in this dream
which is so realistic
    you can almost hear my voice
      at your ear

         which is on the level of your back,
              dear

52

Fish and Cheep Pet Shoppe
The Pioneer
Block Drug   Manhattan
Fox's Corner
Martha's
    are all places I have never visited
      though I keep meaning to

    Italy is a boot in the atlas

        The snowball centuries rolling
        collect only the tiny footprints of
        hens
the burning bush attracts
    the hen

         One comes to take one's
         place in the sun, only
         to smother inside the
         hide of a hen

54

COME IN!

        Hello Lee   Mr. Lee Crabtree

                                of The Fugs

           just came in

55

Rhetoric
is what we make
out of our quarrels
with others

                out of
                our quarrels with ourselves
                we make poetry

        Yes, that is true,

56

                In my house, every cloud
                has a silver lining

      there is only one cloud in my house

Inside that cloud is a joke

        it is not an inside joke

57

on every mirror
in my house
      is a big kiss

        placed there by Mr. Joe Brainard

•

    it's very exciting
        not to be asleep now

            •

            58

If Joe Brainard were here now
he'd be excited
        about giving me those kisses

that's a lie
        clickety-clack   William Saroyan

            59

    What we do in life
    in New York City
        in 1965
    we get the money

            60

                GET THE MONEY!
    that was Damon Runyon's favorite expression

the heat is coming on
like gangbusters
        (A. Partridge
          History of American Climate)

        I guess that means
        it's time to burst,
        eh,
           M'sieur Cloud?

61

Speaking of Picasso, he once sd
      that for him

            true friendship cannot exist
       without the possibility of
         sex

         That is true

   I have many men friends
   I would like to fuck

           However, I am unable to do so
           because I am not a homosexual

fortunately
this makes my life complex
rather than simple
        and vice versa

62

Dream on O impudent virgin
         Guillaume Apollinaire
    you too are aware of the duality of nature and of
the spirit
    and you too prefer the visible
          to the invisible

    I salute You!

       (Salutes)

63

the true Guillaume
is a great deal more interesting
than many of those people
whose misfortune it is
not to be so true

64

$$\text{the logic of that is}$$
lost
but may be recovered
in the theory of Mr. A.N. Whitehead to the effect
that a human being
may possess two kinds of perception / that
as it were
work from opposite ends.
(breathing)

65

So, in conclusion, may I say
that this is what life is like here
you drink some coffee, you get some sleep
everything is up in the air

especially us, who are me

66

Now
in the middle of this
someone I love is dead

and I don't even know
"how"

> I thought she belonged to me

How she filled my life when I felt empty!

How she fills me now!

67

games of cribbage
      with Dick
      filled this afternoon
                          do you
                          understand that?

68

What
     excitement!
           crossing Saint Mark's Place
        face cold in air
          tonight
              when
                    that girlish someone waving
                        from a bicycle
                           turned me back on.

69

What moves me most, I guess
           of a sunlit morning
     is being alone
        with everyone I love
  crossing 6th and 1st
  at ice-cold 6 a.m.

from where I come home
with two French donuts, Pepsi and
the New York Times.

70

Joy is what I like,
That, and love.

4 OCT. 65 — 16 JAN. 66

A DREAM

Dreamy-eyed is how you get
when you need something strong
"in some cup of your own"

The gift of coffee is an act of love
unless it costs you

Love came into my room
I mean my life
the shape of a Tomato
it took over everything

later:

Forgive me, René Magritte
I meant a "a rose"

You have a contemporary nature
in these here coffee alps

I dreamt that December 27th, 1965
while sleeping with Linda Schjeldahl
in a dream

BEAN SPASMS

for George Schneeman

New York's lovely weather
               hurts my forehead

              in praise of thee
                      the? white dead
                      whose eyes know:
          what are they
of the tiny cloud my brain:
The City's tough red buttons:

                  O Mars, red, angry planet, candy

                    bar, with sky on top,
         "why, it's young Leander hurrying to his death"
      what? what time is it in New York   in these here alps
    City of lovely tender hate
              and beauty making beautiful
                    old rhymes?
   I ran away from you
when you needed something strong
      then I leand against the toilet bowl (ack)
    Malcolm X
        I love my brain
  it all mine now is
  saved not knowing
      that &
      that (happily)
      being that:

    "wee kill our selves to propagate our kinde"
                     John Donne
yes, that's true

the hair on yr nuts & my
   big blood-filled cock are a part in that
too

PART 2

 Mister Robert Dylan doesn't feel well today
 That's bad
 This picture doesn't show that
 It's not bad, too

 it's very ritzy in fact

 here I stand I can't stand
  to be thing
I don't use   atop
      the empire state
      building
      & so sauntered out that door
That reminds me of the time
I wrote that long piece about a gangster name of "Jr."
O Harry James! had eyes to wander but lacked tongue to praise
      so later peed under his art

 paused only to lay a sneeze
         on Jack Dempsey
       asleep with his favorite Horse

   That reminds me of I buzz
    on & off Miró pop
      in & out a Castro convertible
minute by minute   GENEROSITY!

 Yes now that the seasons totter in their walk
  I do a lot of wondering about Life in praise of ladies dead of
& Time plaza(s), Bryant Park by the Public   eye of brow
Library, Smith Bros. black boxes, Times
    Square

Pirogi Houses
            with long skinny rivers thru them
they lead the weary away
            off! hey!
                  I'm no sailor
                  off a ship
                              at sea   I'M HERE
                        & "The living is easy"
It's "HIGH TIME"
                        & I'm in shapes
                        of shadow, they
                        certainly can warm, can't they?

            Have you ever seen one?   NO!
                        of those long skinny Rivers
                              So well hung, in New York City
                  NO!   in fact
                              I'm the Wonderer
& as yr train goes by   forgive me, René!   'just oncet'
I woke up in Heaven
                  He woke, and wondered more; how many angels
      on this train huh?   snore

                        for there she lay
            on sheets that mock lust   done that 7 times
                                    been caught
                        and brought back
                  to a peach nobody.

      To Continue:
      Ron Padgett & Ted Berrigan
            hates yr brain
                  my dears
                  amidst the many other little buzzes
      & like, Today, as Ron Padgett might say
                  is

         "A tub of vodka"
                "in the morning"
     she might reply
and that keeps it up
   past icy poles
           where angels beg fr doom then zip
              ping in-and-out, joining the army
      wondering about Life
       by the Public Library of
             Life
                 No Greater Thrill!
     (I wonder)

Now that the earth is changing I wonder what time it's getting to be
    sitting on this New York Times Square
  that actually very ritzy, Lauren   it's made of yellow wood or
           I don't know something   maybe
    This man was my   it's been fluffed up
     friend
          He had a sense for the
            vast   doesn't he?

      Awake my Angel! give thyself
        to the lovely hours   Don't cheat
    The victory is not always to the sweet.
        I mean that.

Now this picture is pretty good here
Though it once got demerits from the lunatic Arthur Cravan
He wasn't feeling good that day
Maybe because he had nothing on
          paint-wise I mean

PART 3

            I wrote that
            about what is
      this empty room   without a heart
            now in three parts
            a white flower
      came home wet & drunk   2 Pepsis
      and smashed my fist thru her window
                              in the nude
      As the hand zips you see
            Old Masters, you can see
      well hung in New York   they grow fast here
            Conflicting, yet purposeful
                  yet with outcry vain!

PART 4

            Praising, that's it!
you string a sonnet around yr fat gut
      and falling on your knees
                        you invent the shoe
                        for a horse. It brings you luck
                  while sleeping
                        "You have it seems a workshop nature"
Have you   "Good Lord!"
                                    Some folks is wood
seen them?   Ron Padgett wd say
                  amidst the many other little buzzes
                  past the neon on & off
                  night & day   STEAK SANDWICH
                  Have you ever tried one Anne?   SURE!
      "I wonder what time 'its'?"
            as I sit on this new Doctor

NO   I only look at buildings they're in
as you and he, I mean he & you & I buzz past
                    in yellow ties   I call that gold
         THE HOTEL BUCKINGHAM
     (facade) is black, and taller than last time
is looming over lunch   naked   high time   poem   & I, equal in
                       perfection & desire
      is looming   two eyes   over coffee-cup (white) nature
          and man: both hell on poetry.
          Art is art and life is
            'A monograph on Infidelity"
      Oh. Forgive me stench of sandwich
      O pneumonia in American Poetry

    Do we have time?   well look at Burroughs
     7 times been caught and brought back to Mars
        & eaten.
"Art is art & Life
is home," Fairfield Porter said that
        turning himself in
           Tonight arrives again in red
some go on   even in Colorado   on the run
        the forests shake
     meaning:
        coffee   the cheerfulness of this poor
              fellow is terrible, hidden in
              the fringes of the eyelids'
     blue mysteries   (I'M THE SKY)
   The sky is bleeding now
       onto 57th Street
     of the 20th Century &
      HORN & HARDART'S

Right Here. That's PART 5

   I'm not some sailor off a ship at sea
I'm the wanderer   (age 4)
     & now everyone is dead
    sinking bewildered of hand, of foot, of lip
 nude, thinking
laughter burnished brighter than hate

           Goodbye.
    André Breton said that
        what a shit!
Now he's gone!
    up bubbles all his amorous breath
   & Monograph on Infidelity entitled
        The Living Dream
I never again played
     I dreamt that December 27th, 1965
    all in the blazon of sweet beauty's breast

  I mean "a rose" Do you understand that?
      Do you?
The rock&roll songs of this earth
commingling absolute joy AND
incontrovertible joy of intelligence
       certainly can warm
      can't they? YES!
   and they do.
  Keeping eternal whisperings around

        (Mr. MacAdams writes in
        the nude: no that's not
(we want to take the underground me that: then zips in &
 revolution to Harvard!)   out the boring taxis, re-
           fusing to join the army
  and yet this girl has   asleep "on the springs"
   so much grace   of red GENEROSITY)
   I wonder!

          Were all their praises simply prophecies
   of this
        the time!   NO GREATER THRILL
            my friends

   But I quickly forget them, those other times, for what are they
  but parts in the silver lining of the tiny cloud my brain
drifting up into smoke the city's tough blue top:

        I think a picture always
         leads you gently to someone else
  Don't you? like when you ask to leave the room
         & go to the moon.

FEBRUARY AIR

for Donna Dennis

Can't cut it (night)

        in New York City

    it's alive

inside my tooth

      on St. Mark's Place

   where exposed nerve

        jangles

     •

that light
isn't on

    for me

      that's it

         though you are
         right here.

    •

   It's RED RIVER
    time
      on tv

and
Andy's BRILLO BOX is on
the icebox is on   High
     too   over St. Nazaire, the
            Commando is poised

that means tonight's raid
is "on"

The Monkey
at the typewriter
is turned on

(but the tooth hurts)

You'd Better Move On . . . .

You'd Better Move On

wake up
smoke pot
see the cat
love my wife
think of Frank

eat lunch
make noises
sing songs
go out
dig the streets

go home for dinner
read the Post
make pee-pee
two kids
grin

read books
see my friends
get pissed-off
have a Pepsi
disappear

SELFLESSNESS

to Peter Schjeldahl

This picture indicates development
You drink some coffee, you get some sleep
Everything is up in the air
especially us

who are me

Linda greets our force
forcefully

so much for that

(sing)
"I'm sittin' here thinkin'
just how sharp I am . . . ."

I ask you, can these words have issued
from M'sieur M. "The Rock" Proust,
BPOE, RSVP, ICUP?

No.

You inhabit a baby, I mean
a table . . .
the logic of that
is lost

is mixed with public opinion
and
as we get closer & closer
something snaps
Music gets into this picture
of
"A Life."

& Now it's rolling . . .

       & Now we are one

       & it's bed-time

                competitive spirits
      dare we continue? we dare continue
    seeking parties
   full of places
we have not been at
       nor ever will be at
           without each other.

MANY HAPPY RETURNS

for Dick Gallup

It's a great pleasure to
wake "up"
   mid-afternoon

      2 o'clock

    and if thy stomach think not

  no matter . . .

     because
     the living
       "it's easy"

      you splash the face &
      back of the neck
    swig Pepsi

  & drape the bent frame in something
       "blue for going out"

     • • •

  you might smoke a little pot, even
    or take a pill
      or two pills

      •

  (the pleasures of prosperity
    tho they are only bonuses
        really
    and neither necessary nor not)

      •

& then:

POOF!

• • •

Puerto-Rican girls are terrific!
                          you have to smile but you don't
                          touch, you haven't eaten
                          yet, & you're too young
                to die . . .

                                    •

No, I'm only kidding!
                Who on earth would kill
                                    for love? (Who wouldn't?)

                                    •

                          Joanne & Jack
                will feed you
                today
because
                Anne & Lewis are
                "on the wing" as
                                    but not like
                                              always . . .

                                    • •

Michael is driving a hard bargain
                          himself
                                    to San Francisco . . .

                                    •

                          &
                Pete & Linda
                & Katie and George,
                          Emilio, Elio and Paul
                                    have all gone to Maine . . .

● ● ●

Everyone, it seems, is somewhere else.
       None are lost, tho. At least,
         we aren't!
                    (GEM SPA: corner of 2nd Avenue &
                             Saint Mark's Place)

●

I'm right here
sunlight opening up the sidewalk,
opening up today's breakfast black&white,
& I'm about to be
born again thinking of you

LIVING WITH CHRIS

for Christina Gallup

It's not exciting to have a bar of soap
in your right breast pocket
it's not boring either
it's just what's happening in America, in 1965

If there is no Peace in the world
it's because there is no Peace
in the minds of men. You'd be surprised, however
at how much difference
a really good cup of coffee & a few pills can make
in your day

I would like to get hold of
the owner's manual
for a 1965 model " DREAM"
(Catalogue number CA-77)

I am far from the unluckiest woman in the world

I am far from a woman

An elephant is tramping in my heart

Alka-Seltzer   Palmolive   Pepsodent   Fab
Chemical New York

There is nothing worse than elephant love

Still, there is some Peace in the world. It is
night. You are asleep. So I must be at peace

The barometer at 29.58 and wandering

But who are you?

For god's sake, is there anyone out there listening?

If so, Peace.

FRANK O'HARA'S QUESTION
FROM "WRITERS AND ISSUES"
BY JOHN ASHBERY

what sky
out there is between the ailanthuses
a 17th century prison an aardvark
a photograph of Mussolini and
a personal letter from Isak Dinesen
written after eating

can be succeeded by a calm evaluation
of the "intense inane" that surrounds
him:

it is cool
I am high
and happy
as it turns
on the earth
tangles me
in the air

and between these two passages (from
the long poem 'Biotherm') occurs a me-
diating line which might stand to charac-
terize all of Mr. O'Hara's art:

I am guarding it from mess and message.

THINGS TO DO IN NEW YORK CITY

for Peter Schjeldahl

Wake up high up
    frame bent & turned on
Moving slowly
    & by the numbers
light cigarette
Dress in basic black
    & reading a lovely old man's book:

BY THE WATERS OF MANHATTAN

change

    flashback

play cribbage on the Williamsburg Bridge
watching the boats sail by
the sun, like a monument,
move slowly up the sky
above the bloody rush:

break yr legs & break yr heart
kiss the girls & make them cry
loving the gods & seeing them die

        celebrate your own
      & everyone else's birth:

      Make friends forever
      & go away

RESOLUTION

The ground is white with snow.
It's morning, of New Year's Eve, 1968, & clean
City air is alive with snow, it's quiet
Driving. I am 33. Good Wishes, brothers, everywhere

& Don't You Tread On Me.

A Boke
1966

"Poetry."

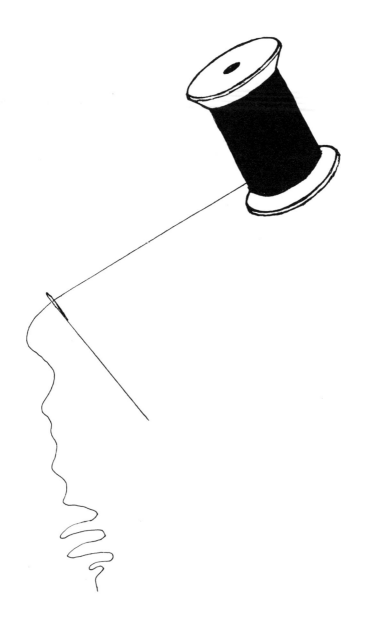

A BOKE

for Dick Gallup

You're listening to a man who in 1964 un-
knowingly breathed in a small quantity of
LSD powder, remember the fragrance of Grandma's
kitchen? — and at a college he reads, sleeps.
The next morning he
takes a walk around the campus
with a young student who is
ordinarily mild-mannered and agree-
able and secretly thinks of him-
self as rather colorless and uninterest-
ing. He has written poems for years,
odd sensation indeed, only partly alleviated
when he learns that he is next door to
the bashed-out windows, is now
engaged in beating in the
top of a car with the inaccurate
ones relieving him. He learns to
time his words and lines to the
hammer-strokes, and before long
he is giving something. And the
grave, slightly puzzled sym-
pathetic faces take on expressions he is
grateful for.
The head picks up. He is taken
to a room in one of the girls'
dormitories, which gives him
a local airline. This is a
girls' college, also
far off in the country. He finds
this out by the use of drugs outside

medical auspices. He and his
followers seem to feel
that the end justifies the means, but
they have no flair (!), and at that moment
the image of his great predecessor,
the only predecessor, Laurence Sterne,
and everything that came into his
head insulted somebody—merciful
heavens, who on earth was it?—and
what the hell, he thinks, this may be
a major technical breakthrough for me.
In that company he thinks he hears a bearded
fellow mutter something discontented about
"a lack of fire" or was he a
singer, an American poet? When at last
he reaches the station he discovers
he is too early by 20 minutes
blazes up humiliatingly in the front
of his brain. The result of this was
that he deliberately drank twice as
there are few lights on the campus, remember
Grandma's kitchen?, and he is uncertain about the
instructions designed to get him into
Literary Vaudeville. At the outset of the
trip he had thought that
the songs themselves would be enough
so had a terrible hangover the next day.
Yet he has in some obscure way
been a good deal better satisfied with
powerful vagueness. Poetry. A car
stops. It is driven
by a student at the college
he is going to, and, ever cognizant
of his bodiless staring audience, and of
the skull beneath his own skin

he has taken to doing some curious
things. For example he has acquired a
guitar, which he carries about with
Robert Frost and Dylan Thomas; he has
had nothing to complain of as to
the size and response of his audience on
this tour—set up by the editor of a ven-
erable poetry magazine—has dinner
with them, recounts some of his
adventures. Everyone from the schools.
But he is still bothered by the
difference and the inevitability of
death. He has tried for years to
formulate his relationship to these
things and to say something about
how to get to bus and train stations
and airports. He keeps opening
his eyes in his sleep—for what he
has become on this trip bears but little relation
to the self he left
at home in the mind, say, of his wife.
He is, in fact, in the middle of
a tour of readings. So far, considering,
he is not looking forward to acquiring
the courage to get drunk *before*
readings. He is exhausted and exalted
as he has never been, and now, standing
here, these affairs may be mandatory (in
some cases.) Then too many of the schools
like this one, though far back, seemed pleased by
the way things have gone; there have
even been some letters of appreciation,
female voices. There are many
furtive amused glances at him and
he replies in kind but because he liked

to write them, but he has never thought
of them as participating in
a public act, a kind
appeal to girls, and he even
entertains the idea of sneaking
back to his room and dashing
hard on his nerves. He might live
more vividly in this condition
but he cannot write in it.
He is happy and grinning; he feels
resourceful, foolish, and
lucky. "America," he says aloud
about this. He takes out his two
volumes of poetry, and his
manuscript for a third book,
his *Memento Mori,* the great themes
of poetry hit him squarely: the
possibility of love in
these students just coming from
the auditorium sees him approach-
ing with his ragged books
in the center of a new reality—in
this case a cold sleepless room—
he looks at these things from the last
girl's unexpected kiss, the student
with the nine pound ham-
mer—he rearranges his evening's program
around the themes of love and
death, dangerous to the psychological
stability he expects of himself.
He has several misadventures to
lance between what is on the
page, put there by him at odd
beyond-himself moments, and . . .

and the faces. In the middle
guise of fiction, he becomes fascinatingly
alive, living up to the
"giving-them-what-they-want," or might
be expected to feel entitled to
from a poet, beside himself, who
has drunk very much at six or eight
schools before that one part.
Intensity, he murmurs, where have
you been all my life.
He settles down for a sleep
with a young professor who
writes poems and is en-
thusiastic and companionable. He
reads, has a drink at an untidy
bundle of railroads, bus, and airline schedules
marked with a red pencil and
various notes to himself. That
such nervous excitement, such
over-responsiveness to people
is probably the poet's sole
evening repast, and if he
tasted of a wild boar or a stag
which he had roasted in the
cold light coming in from the chapel
tower across the campus, well, remember
the fragrance? There is
only one bus out of town,
he reaches for it, rock-and-roll
music bursts in his face. Rather than
fool with trying to shut it off he pulls
out his manuscripts. One whispers to
another. Though he is a little
afraid to, he admits who he is,

alone in a room with his skull.
In *this* reading, for once in his
life, he feels a correct balance
in his Hamlet, lost somewhere in
the snows of Northern Wisconsin:
he is, eternal strangeness!, a wandering
pose, full of life through thick
glasses. He finishes, stands
glaring for a moment in another
world with fatigue, one who has spent the most
satisfying part of a long tripping
movement that is not really for him, no, it is
for an exhausted hammerer, or for a new
arrival home and he is more
than a little glad of that: they are
wearing out the plug, feeling that he
has had his revenge. He turns on
the light and dresses, not quite able
to stall, asks suddenly, "May I
kiss you?" She agrees without thinking and
she does so with a distinct sense of
quitting while he is ahead. The
applause is long and loud, as if he were
a Beatle. He reaches a stage,
mounts, looks at the last of all clocks,
and leaves. It is 5:15 a.m. It is
time. He gets up out of bed and stumbles just
as he steps down from the stage into a
wave of feathery sweatered girls, a memorable
thing. No doubt. He gives the best reading of his
life, one that will shortly thereafter
have entered a twilight state characterized
by fantastic imagery. He subs a condition
of character and environment in order to

produce alternative modes of behavior.
He sits down, closes his eyes. Time is
annihilated; the bus driver stumbles
aboard, opens a door to a bridge. Finally
someone stops him, a farmer, and takes him 20
miles down the road. The farmer turns off
the highway, one is much interested in his
being there walking across the campus.
He hears a loud gust of many grunts, a crowd
of muffled students cheers him on; it
is fun in the country and there is
nothing to do. Still he is pleasantly
gratified at the turnouts and at the time,
picks up his bags and manuscripts and
his symbolic white guitar, and goes out
into the white darkness.
What is his life like? Where will he die?
Who is this nun giving him a calm
sense of proportion? and who leaves him; and
this time he is really in a
deserted landscape with dead corn in the
building and no one knows him—
"Come home." And who is that thin
serious boy with the crewcut?
In a station wagon they drive together
40 miles into the rainforests. He is
given a room in a cavern, and
gifts; disturbing gifts, perhaps inept
inadequate gifts, but gifts just the
same. He feels that he is overcome.
He is middle-aged, beginning to lose
teeth and hair. He is lishing them
in his mind, down steps.
The next morning he catches a strange

madness; took hold of him first at the
reading when he discovered that
everything he said was being noted and
commented upon. Too, it is a midwinter
night in the midwest, and a man is
lying alone in a sterling ardor.
The next place is a branch of a state
of mind located in the fields in an
inept scarecrow's life. A few big birds
puff and hunch on the telephone wires;
a strange room. On the dresser beside
the complicated clock-radio that
is supposed to wake him on time, there is
an industrial district of a large city.
There he is to be met at the bus station
though it is plain that there is no other
human being in those streets. In a bar,
(ah yes, he needs a drink badly), on
the stairs of a bus, he collapses.
When he wakes up the bus is in
the terminal of the next city. He gets
a small dose, about one-thousandth
the size of an aspirin, and the no-
toriety is definitely agreeable and
he does his best to try to live up to it.
What in fact is his problem? A friend
will drive him to the next
engagement which is
his last. They start out and he pays
and gets out, scarcely knowing what he is
doing but feeling a little better
standing on the hood of a 1953 Buick
with a John Henry type hammer
in his hands, they having a kind of

metric as he adjusts his delivery more and
more to the inevitable banging. Presumes
there is nothing unscientific in
his desire to change the best
proportions of strength and beauty. His
tastes were modest, a piece of bread,
a draught of water, and you were
often sent to drive him out of his
college. "I couldn't believe you'd
be the one I was looking for," the poet
says in another city, where he has
a friend he can stay with a day or two.
He flies in watching the lights of the
city, and in a phrase the losses endured
by everyone every day—the negation of
possibility that occurs each time
we pass anyone's house.
He eats dinner with the writing and the
phrases stay with him when he wakes.
He notes them down and moves on to the
next stop via the bus station. Crossing
the campus on the one path he
knows he keeps reminding himself of
what he is doing. It is ominous that
the only other large institution in
the town is
the state insane asylum. In all, it
is a strangely good occasion.
He leaves that night, paces back and forth.
There is a skull on his table and suddenly
at the sight of it he starts reading.
From the airless close-packed winter bus
station he tries to call his contact at
the noon reading. The tour is to take place that

day and he has four hours to go 40 miles. The
tenuous noise of revolutions and
student demonstrations combine with assembly
lines that will annihilate the miles,
he becoming then an older and more
dependable self, and yet, remembering.
Perhaps though some recent poems about
his children will do the trick. He reads
these quietly and has
inevitable parties given after his
readings, he plays one or two songs,
and then scuttles back into his corner,
realizing now that role-playing is
shameful beside the feelings he
has experienced. Now he has the sensation
that he must calm down and work.
But on the aircraft aimed at last at
his home, he feels also
interested in Yeats' occult pre-
occupations, a curious object to discuss
in good health, far from the poems them-
selves. "Just be yourself," he told him-
self in the beginning. Ah, but
what self? The self develops a full-
blown psychosis. Delusions set in,
along with restlessness; a sensation of
suffocation, withdrawal, excitation, satisfaction,
that he has done the something
idiosyncratic that people are expecting and
that much more, too.
It is more than he wants to pay, and, caught
up by a daring all or nothing plan,
he wants to tell, he does tell the driver to
take him to the high car, thinking

of the open road, the dear love of
comrades, Hart Crane. The long trip
back. He is instantly surrounded.
Someone points him in a direction
and he begins walking with students
trailing him as though he is un-
comfortable, even desperate: he is
sure he has not written any poetry that
would turn him around.
It begins to snow. Traffic
slows all around
him for miles. Finally a lucky kind of
exhilaration has come over him
and he sings with
white breath to the passing hours, followed by
complete recovery the next day.
He pulls out the packet of schedules:
something is wrong. He has forgotten
that his after-words are being received almost
as things, and toward the end he comes to
think that the things have the quality of a
college, but cannot reach him. He hails a
cab and asks the fare to the town he is going
to with a certain condescending benevolence,
and begins.
It is over. He relaxes with the
faculty party and goes to bed.
He dreams he is a scarecrow in a field
and writes poems
in his head all night. Some few
believe he is where he is: some place in
Wisconsin, where he has given a
poetry reading at a small college; he
has never been lionized by anyone,

not even his immediate family; but
these small repeated tastes of local
mints continue; he bellows louder and
louder and the flinching
audience is with him to the end of a couple
of things modelled on Walter Benton's
"This is my Beloved."
If they were good, and he read them well,
he could collect his money at
each stop with a clear
conscience. An hour goes by. He considers various
alternatives, but they are all
as absurd as the wish to grow
wings. Besides, another hammering is going on.
When an especially loud cheer comes in from
outside he looks up, thinking, "What is wrong
with such and such a concept?" Students
gather round him afterwards, pressing
their manuscripts into his hands,
telling him that the college he is to read in that
night is denominational. He goes up to the
priest, who has been in fact pointing to the right
direction all along. Remember now? He is now standing
alone in the snow, in a strange state, hitch-hiking.
He is 45 years old. For better or for
worse he has been moving and speaking among his kind.
But it is he who is not satisfied with this.
Remember the fragrance of Grandma's kitchen? It is not
only poetry that is
involved, it is the poet as well. Vastly he resolves
to see if he can work something out
about this later, on the bus, at a reasonable hour.
He rides calmly back to a city within a
city, with a certain flair now, since he has forgotten

to telegraph his arrival. No one meets him at the
airport, he phones a friend in the city for a day
and a night before flying home. He sees the
people who sponsored as much liquor as he is
accustomed to at a party after the reading,
waves his arms wildly about and says, "Anything
amounts to something!" And, looking at his watch, he
turns it one way and another so his thin hands can catch
the keys. He has not played the
guitar for years but feels immediately
all out and looks around for whoever is
supposed to help him. There is no one
but a priest, and finally it happens.
One of them, a girl, not the one he would
have picked to pen such a thing, is already
half an hour late. They all reach
the college, then the building, a crowd-raising
scheme by some clod or other.
All through the reading all sorts of new and
poetic things happen to him. Each time he carries
it to another campus. At a turn he gets off
his freeway; they are not so far from the
college as they thought but he
was not gracefully but dis-
gracefully drunk, who is now halfway into a new frankness.
"I couldn't believe in you, either," says the
priest with candor. Riveting him with
astonishment, directly in front of the
building, a lanky student comes out of the
building and talks to him an hour or two before
dinner. He lies down on a bed, then gets up,
is finished. He finds his poems,
usually rather loose in rhythm, taking
on a thumping thunderment and

incoherent babbling. These symptoms lasted
several decades. Actually they have been
responded to to a degree he has come to
consider excessive and even manic, but he
suspects that attendance at college seems to
be all but inaccessible. There are no
buses or trains until after time confers her
particular favors on a stranger she
will never see again, one who last night
grew more emotional, more harried, more
impulsive. Yet he knows that these qualities
will die out, take a wrong turn somewhere.
On a highway complex as big as this one
it is hard to get tween his touring self and
his usual self. He has definitely been
another person.

Waterloo Sunset
1964–1968

"one foot
is expressing itself as continuum
the other, sock"

IN THREE PARTS

According
to
the
basic
law
of
visual
perception
any
stimulus
pattern
tends
to
be
seen
in
such
a
way
that
the
resulting
pattern
is
as
simple
as
the
given
conditions
permit.

*

Before
the
orgasmic
platform
in
the
outer
third
of
the
vagina
develops
sufficiently
to
provide
increased
exteroceptive
and
proprioceptive
stimulation
for
both
sexes,
the
over-
distended
excitement-
phase
vagina
gives
many
women
the
sensation

that
the
fully
erect
penis
is
"lost
in
the
vagina."

*

With
daring
and
strength
men
like
Pollock,
deKooning,
Tobey,
Rothko,
Smith
and
Kline
filled
their
work
with
the
drama,
anger,
pain,
and

confusion
of
contemporary
life.

WATERLOO SUNSET

We ate lunch, remember? and I paid the check
Under trees in rain of false emotion and big bull
With folks going in and out putting words in our mouths that are
shouting, "Hurrah for Bristol Cream!" We threw a leave-sandwich
Into the sunlight-it greedily gobbled it up, and growing brighter
Emanating from their glasses came the little drinkies
Reflections of the magazine Grandma edits
On whose pages a bouquet is blossoming sort of. You bounced a check
Into years of lives down under the weather vane, barf!
The influence of alcohol rebounded 500 miles into Africa.

But a little drinkie never hurt nobody, except an African.
The Earth sops up liquids, I mean drinks,
And is tipsy as pinballs on the ocean
Wobbling on its axis. We turn a paleface shade of white
In the rain that pelts the doo-doo
That flies from the eyes' blinds. It doesn't matter though
                    on the sweet side
Of the moon. Don't be a horrible sourpuss
Moon! Have a drink
Have an entire issue! Waves goodbye & reels, into sun
Of light dark light roll over Beethoven
Our shelter-half misses your shelter-half. There's nothing left
                    of love
But we have checkerberry leaves
Mint, Juniper, tree-light
Elder-flowers, sweet goldenrod, bugspray & Juice.

And you are a pretty girl-boy
And I am a pretty man-woman
and we are here-there
In England and the food is absolutely cold-hot.

In the aromatic sundown, according to the magazine version
Or automatic sundown   English words are a gas
Slurring the Earth's one heaving angel turns in unison
& paddles your rear gently as befits one in love
          with you & I
No change   My face is all right

For us. We are bored through & we are through with you
With our professionalism (you have to become useless to drink).

All we ever wanted to do in the rosy sunlight was
In the first place was . . . was . . . was . . . uh
Run our fingers through your curly hair
Oooops! No, not that. I mean all
We really wanted to do was jazz yr mother
Fight off insects & sing a sad solitary tune
On the excellencies of Bristol Cream
Six dollars a bottle Praise The Lord!

—TED BERRIGAN & RON PADGETT

AMERICAN EXPRESS

Cold rosy dawn in New York City
                              not for me
in Ron's furlined Jim Bridger
                              (coat)
that I borrowed two years ago
                              had cleaned
but never returned, Thank god!
                              On 6th Street
Lunch poems burn
                 a hole is in my pocket
two donuts one paper bag
                     in hand
hair is in my face and in my head is
                     "cold rosy dawn in New York City"

I woke up this morning
                     it was night
you were on my mind
                     on the radio
And also there was a letter
                     and it's to you
if "you" is Ron Padgett,
                     American express
shivering now in Paris
                     Oklahoma
two years before
                 buying a new coat for the long trip
back to New York City
                 that I'm wearing now

It is cold in here
                 for two

looking for the boll weevil
                    (looking for a home), one with pimples
one blonde, from Berkeley
                    who says, "Help!" and
"Hey, does Bobby Dylan come around here?"
                                        "No, man," I say,
"Too cold!"
            & they walk off, trembling,
                              (as I do in L.A.)
so many tough guys, faggots, & dope addicts!
                                though I assure them
"Nothing like that in New York City!"
                        It's all in California!
(the state state)
            that shouldn't be confused with
                              The balloon state
that I'm in now
            hovering over the radio
                    following the breakfast of champions
& picking my curious way
                    from left to right
                              across my own white
                    expansiveness

MANHATTAN!

      listen
  The mist of May
              is on the gloaming
& all the clouds
            are halted, still
                        fleecy
            & filled
                        with holes.
  They are alight with borrowed warmth,
                              just like me.

DICK GALLUP (BIRTHDAY)

(for the Gallups)

interrupts yr privacy

25 years later

> you wait between the dodge and the bush
> a basket
> between you and your arm: under it

INSIGHT (Vol. 1, Nr. 3)

> (the condemned man is shielding a
> woman, about 25, five feet
> eleven inches high, hair dark, curly,
> dark eyes; and though not gallant, is pure . . .

the street disappearing
into bush level
two heads above the basket

> ("seeking a person-
> al world, where one's own
> behavior has a code . . .

is no guarantee
of justice, folks.

SUNLIGHT IN
JUNGLE-LAND

● ●

that girl wreathed in blue
and that one, in yellow

corporeal

"her hair a wondrous gold"

        MAIN-TRAVELED ROADS'
(under the sheets)

                           the community
in their vicinity, is murder.
It keeps us awake.

FOLK LEGENDS do not await Verdicts.

We get on, with provisions.
It (The Dodge) continues.

LIFE AMONG THE WOODS

Near Paris, there is a boat. Near this boat live the beautiful Woods.

They are a charming family, the Woods, very friendly: Mr.Woods, Mrs.Woods, their son Peter, and their tiny daughter, Bubbles.

Mr.Woods is very rich. He has a grand house, in four pieces: a kitchen, a stable, a room for lying down, and a room for infants. In this house there is, in addition, a brain room.

Mr.Woods' garden is also very grand. It is full of lettuces, flowers and fruits.

Mrs.Woods likes cooking plenty. She makes pies, pots of tea, and desserts. The little Woods have beautiful appetites. They eat a lot.

Mrs. Woods' kitchen is very appropriate. It has a pretty little furnace, a table, four chaise lounges and a large placard. On the placard there are six S's, six tassels, and fifty soupspoons. (One of the soupspoons is crusty.) There is also a grand casserole.

In the room for laying down there are four tiny books, four chaise lounges and four tiny tables. One sometimes goes to the toilet on the tables.

In the room for infants there is a big table, plenty of chaise lounges and one grand placard on which are pictures of the toys of the tiny Woods: a puppy, a train, a toupee, a cigarette, some balls, some books, a pellet, soap, a strangler's cord, and lots of other things.

The black bag and the wise man may be found in the brain room.

They eat in the stable, where there is a grand table and some chaise lounges.

Mrs.Woods' rat poison is kept in the stable, in a great bottle.

In her office she keeps plenty of other things. She keeps bread, berries, beer, lace, celery, buttons, plums, and a comforter.

THE TEN GREATEST
BOOKS OF THE YEAR (1967)

Apollinaire Oeuvres Poetiques
Swami Sivananda, Waves of Bliss
James Joyce, Ulysses
Gerard Malanga & Andy Warhol, Screen Test/A Diary
The Collected Earlier Poems of William Carlos Williams
Helen Hathaway, What Your Voice Reveals
Jean Jacques Mayoux, Melville
Kay Ambrose, Ballet-Lovers Pocketbook
Roger Shattuck, Apollinaire
William Shakespeare, Cymbeline
Charlin's Anglo-French Course 3rd Part
The Pocket Dictionary of Art Terms
Locus Solus No. 2
Compositions Property of Ted Berrigan
Jack Kerouac, Mexico City Blues
Ron Loewinsohn, L'Autre
Ted Berrigan, Clear The Range
Philip Whalen, Selfportrait From Another Direction
Wallace Stevens, Collected Poems
The Complete Sonnets Songs and Poems of William Shakespeare
Boswell's Life of Johnson
The Collected Later Poems of William Carlos Williams
The Oxford Book of English Verse
Williams & Macy, Do You Know English Literature
Richard Brautigan, Trout Fishing In America
Jim Carroll, Organic Trains
Stokely Carmichael, Toward Black Liberation
Ted Berrigan, The Sonnets
Ted Berrigan & Ron Padgett, Bean Spasms
Dick Gallup, The Lungs of Sophocles
Eduardo Paolozzi, Kex

Eduardo Paolozzi, Kex
Lawrence Campbell, Sills
Diter Rot, Buch
Ted Berrigan, Art Notes
Velversheen by Eagle-A
Ron Padgett, Tone Arm
Poetry Magazine May 1960
University Note Book
Jim Brodey, Clothesline
The Cantos of Ezra Pound CX-CXVI
Frank O'Hara, Meditations In An Emergency
Walt Whitman, Leaves of Grass
David Henderson, Felix of the Silent Forest
Poets of the English Language Vol. III Milton to Goldsmith
Poets of the English Language Vol. I Langland to Spenser
Poets of the English Language Vol. V Tennyson to Yeats
Fuck You, A Magazine of the Arts Vol. 6, No. 5
The World No. 7
William Burroughs, Time
Folder No. 2
Larry McMurtry, The Last Picture Show
"C" Comics

FRAGMENT

for Jim Brodey

Left behind in New York City, & oof!
That's the right one: sitting now, & I'm not thinking
Nor swishing; I'm just sitting. Getting over them two
Hamburgers.   & that I think
Gets it all down. Here, anyway, I am
On this electric chair each breath nearer the last
Oceans of ripples solid under me: how come?
One pair of time-capsules trigger sweat
As one listens & one listening type types
LOOKS LIKE WE GONNA GET A LITTLE SNOW, HUH?
I don't know but you can bet something's going
     to happen.

5 NEW SONNETS : A POEM

for Barry & Jacky Hall

1.

His piercing pince-nez. Some dim frieze
dear Berrigan. He died
I, an island, sail, and my shores toss
to breathe an old woman slop oatmeal,
My babies parade waving their innocent flags
The taste of such delicate thoughts
Opulent, sinister, and cold!
Sing in idiom of disgrace
Dreams, aspirations of presence! Innocence gleaned,
annealed! The world in its mysteries are explained
On the grass. To think of you alone
Your champion. Days are nursed on science fiction
For the fey Saint's parade   Today
Rivers of annoyance undermine the arrangements.

2.

Hands point to a dim frieze, in the dark night.
Back to books. I read
on a fragrant evening, fraught with sadness
bristling hate.
And high upon the Brooklyn Bridge alone,
Huddled on the structured steps
The bulbs burn, phosphorescent, white,
Shall it be male or female in the tub?
Pale like an ancient scarf, she is unadorned,
and the struggles of babies congeal. A hard core is formed.
Suffering the poem of these states!
& you tremble at the books upon the earth
& he walks. Three ciphers and a faint fakir
No.   One   Two   Three   Four   Today

3.

It's 8:30 p.m. in New York and I've been running
Wind giving presence to fragments.
at every hand, my critic
Flinging currents into pouring streams
The bulbs burn phosphorescent, white
Fathers and Teachers and Daemons down under the sea,
The singer sleeps in Cos. Strange juxtaposed
"I wanted to be a cowboy." Doughboy will do
As my strength and I walk out and look for you
Winds flip down the dark path of breath
Released by night (which is not to imply   clarity
She is warm. Into the closed air of the slow
The wind's wish is the tree's demand
On the 15th day of November in the year of the motorcar.

4.

Is there room in the room that you room in?
How much longer shall I be able to inhabit the divine
deep in whose reeds great elephants decay;
loveliness that longs for butterfly! There is no pad
He buckles on his gun, the one
He wanted to know the *names*
And the green rug nestled against the furnace
Your hair moves slightly,
He is incomplete, bringing you Ginger Ale
The cooling wind keeps blowing, and
He finds he cannot fake
Wed to wakefulness, night which is not death
Fuscous with murderous dampness
But helpless, as blue roses are helpless.

& 5

Into the closed air of the slow
And then one morning to waken perfect-faced
The blue day! In the air winds dance
Sleep half sleep half silence and with reason
banging around in a cigarette   she isn't "in love"
In my paintings for they are present
The withered leaves fly higher than dolls can see
A watchdog barks in the night
Francis Marion nudges himself gently into the big blue sky
What thwarts this fear I love
No lady dream around in any bad exposure
absence of passion, principles, love. She murmurs
Is not genuine   it shines forth from the faces
littered with soup, cigarette butts, the heavy

21 MAY 1970

POOP

after Francis Picabia

Nature makes my teeth "to hurt"

*

Each conviction lengthens the sentence

*

Women are interesting when I look at them

*

Art is medicine for imbeciles

*

Great Art is a Great Mistake

*

If it's inspiration you want, drop your panties

*

If I fall in love with my friend's wife, she's fucked*

                    *alternates:

                             I'm fucked
                             he's fucked

bent

interstices

30

The fucking enemy shows up

CENTO: A NOTE ON PHILOSOPHY

for Pat Mitchell

When I search the past for you
We who are the waiting fragments of his sky
"I who am about to die"
Then was the drowsy melody of languish
And staying like white water; and now of a sudden
A too resilient mind
Cajoling, scheming, scolding, the cleverest of them all
And so we ride together into the peach state!
(Remain secure from pain preserve thy hate thy heart)

Those are the very rich garments of the poor
The rack and the crucifix of winter, winter's wild
Which encases me. What about the light that comes in then?
Silence; and in between these silences
The spins and the flowing of night-time.
Praising, that's it! One ordained to praise
The wind without flesh, without bone
The morning-glory, climbing the morning long
In ordinary places.
Not to mention the chief thing

We think by feeling. What is there to know?
Bouncing a red rubber ball in the veins
Though my ship was on the way it got caught in some moorings
Melodic signs of Arabic adventure
Darting into a tender fracas leeward and lee
The fields breathe sweet, the daisies kiss our feet
And you have made the world (and it shall grow)
The last the sole surviving Texas Ranger
The heavy not which you were bringing back alone
Abandoned, almost Dionysian

Why should I climb the look-out?
The child who has fallen in love with maps and charts
Drums in the pre-dawn. In my head my brain
But to be part of the treetops and the blueness, invisible
In red weather.

Questions, oh, I hope they do not find you
I go on loving you like water, but
I am in love with poetry. Every way I turn
I think I am bicycling across an Africa of green and white fields
Into a symbol. I hate that. I falter. These

Let the snake wait under
My back, for which act
I would not credit comment upon gracefully
How how the brig brig water the damasked roses
But helpless, as blue roses are helpless
The revolution is done. What has a bark, but cannot bite?
I've tucked the rushing earth under my legs
By those, to sing of cleanly wantonesse
To walk, and pass long love's day.

"It is such a beautiful day I had to write you a letter
On along the street. Somewhere a trolley, taking leave
Just to be leaving; hearts light as balloons
mirrored in little silver spoons."
True voyagers alone are those who leave
The falcon cannot hear the falconer
They never shrink from their fatality
Upon those under lands, the vast
And, without knowing why, say, "Let's get going! Goodbye."
& so, sauntered out that door, which was closed.

THE TEN GREATEST
BOOKS OF THE YEAR, 1968

The Collected Earlier Poems by William Carlos Williams
Selected Writings Charles Olson
Chicago Review One Dollar
Alkahest
New American Writing No. 1
THE RANDOM HOUSE DICTIONARY OF THE ENGLISH LANGUAGE
The Pocket Aristotle
After Dinner We take A Drive Into The Night by Tony Towle
Love Poems (Tentative Title) by Frank O'Hara
The Sky Pilot in No Man's Land by Ralph Connors
Cosmic Consciousness by Dr. Richard Bucke
Meditations On The Signs of The Zodiac by John Jocelyn

In Public In Private by Edwin Denby

The World Number 1	Cover by Dan Clark
The World Number 2	Cover by Robert McMillan
The World Number 3	Cover by George Schneeman
The World Number 4	Cover by Donna Dennis
The World Number 5	Cover by Jack Boyce
The World Number 6	Cover by Fielding Dawson
The World Number 7	Cover by Bill Beckman
The World Number 8	Cover by George Schneeman
The World Number 9	Cover by Joe Brainard
The World Number 10	Cover by Larry Fagin
The World Number 11	Cover by Tom Clark
The World Number 12	Cover by George Schneeman
The World Number 13	Cover by Donna Dennis
The World Number 14	Cover by Joe Brainard

from THE ART OF THE SONNET

for Tom Clark

1.

It is a very great thing
To call across the room
To a girl,
"Hey, I love you."

You shout very loudly.
A lot of weird freaky people
Look at you very strangely plus assorted boring square types—
The girl does not hear you.

She is puce, and yellow. You are completely ass
Because the girl you are yelling to is Whistler's Mother.
PS: You are also somewhat color-blind.
Or could it be that you are The Joker, my plum-blossomed Visionary

Friend? Those tiny broken veins on the tip of your nose are
Tres interesting. They resemble the map of Crete.

2.

Some of Denis Roche's books are missing here.
Let's go out. We can go to the park.
Dead Fingers Talk. They say, "I got some books here
That we can steal things out of.

They're all by good writers." Silence.
Orange Juice. Five dog barks then another.
Then too many to count shut up you dumb mutt.
In Korea they give puppies to GI's who fatten them up

---

from THE ART OF THE SONNET

for Tom Clark

1.

It is a very great thing
To call across the room
To a girl,
"Hey, I love you."

You shout very loudly.
A lot of weird freaky people
Look at you very strangely plus assorted boring square types—
The girl does not hear you.

She is puce, and yellow. You are completely ass
Because the girl you are yelling to is Whistler's Mother.
PS: You are also somewhat color-blind.
Or could it be that you are The Joker, my plum-blossomed Visionary

Friend? Those tiny broken veins on the tip of your nose are
Tres interesting. They resemble the map of Crete.

2.

Some of Denis Roche's books are missing here.
Let's go out. We can go to the park.
Dead Fingers Talk. They say, "I got some books here
That we can steal things out of.

They're all by good writers." Silence.
Orange Juice. Five dog barks then another.
Then too many to count shut up you dumb mutt.
In Korea they give puppies to GI's who fatten them up

Then they steal them back to make soup. Ack.
I think we oughtta write a great poem outta these books.
That dog is still barking. My stomach is growling: Ravi Shankar
I got all great books here to write poems from.

Maybe we could write a sonnet. Great burst of applause:
Ladies & Gentlemen, it's all about to happen, & now it's done.

3.

I've been loving you a little too long.
I can't stop now. Why should I stop now?
You don't know, do you? I think it is very nice
Of you. Incidentally, I went to the fortune teller

She looked into the crystal ball. She saw
Two New York Yankees & they were very small.
I left there in a hurry. I needed one pall mall.
I got one from a midget. It was long as he was tall.

In case you haven't figured it out, Lady of Mondrian, the lake
I made up most of the above. You see, I did it
Because I'm a nut. Yet, isn't it all right to be sort of nutty, a flake,
When you are in love? Why not

Call me up sometime?
212-677-7779.

IN 4 PARTS

for John Giorno

A person can lie around on an uncrowded beach

And when too much peace and quiet gets on his
nerves, he can always get dressed and tour Israel.

*

Mayor
Frank
X.
Graves
today
ordered
the
arrest
of
Allen
Ginsberg
if
the
police
could
prove
that
the
poet
smoked
marijuana
while
looking
at
the

Passaic
Falls
yesterday.

*

The
Jewish
Memorial
Hospital's
Junior
League
will
give
its
second
annual
discotheque
benefit
Sunday
at
the
Round
Table.

*

William
Carlos
Williams
the
Paterson
N.J.
physician
was
a
strong

and
vigorous
poet
who
spoke
in
the
American
idiom.

ENTRANCE

for Ed Dorn

10 years of boot
Take it away
& it's off
Under the table
    2
   & I'm hovering
I'm above *American Language*
                     one foot
is expressing itself as continuum
the other, sock

groan   I am dog
    tired from cake
walking
    to here.   That is,
    An Entrance.

So Going Around Cities
1968–1969

"Whole days went by, and later their years"
— Frank O'Hara

GREY MORNING

for Alice Notley

Rain
Coming down
Outside her
Windows
I can be seen inside
                    the drops
                    of rain
                    falling
                    limping
                    This girl in mind.

AUTUMN

Autumn is fun

for these kids

who love me

But comes a Voyeur

W / his champagne

to this tub

It shrinks

       disappears.

The pills aren't working.

ANTI-WAR POEM

for Robert Harris

It's New Year's Eve, of 1968, & a time
for Resolution.

I don't like Engelbert Humperdink.

I love the incredible String Band.

The War goes on
                    & war is Shit.

I'll sing you a December song.

It's 5 below zero in Iowa City tonight.

This year I found a warm room
That I could go to
                    be alone in
& never have to fight.

I didn't live in it.

I thought a lot about dying
But I said *Fuck it.*

POEM

of morning, Iowa City, blue
gray & green out the window . . .
A mountain, blotchy pink & white
is rising, breathing, smoke

Now, lumbering, an Elephant, on
crutches, is sailing; down
Capitol, down Court, across
Madison & down College, cold
  clear air
         pouring in

        Now those crutches
are being tossed aside; the
Elephant is beginning to rise
into the warm regulated air
        of another altitude

That air is you, your breathing

Thanks for it, & thanks a lot
for Pasternak: The Poems of Yurii Zhivago
& Mayakovsky: Poems.
         They were great.

         Now it's me.

HERE I LIVE

So   sleeping & waking
    every day

        up

I live here   I,

            the great
            mumbling

                    one

        two   three   four

Laid out,   voices   living & dead

            hovering

                    between

    heart   &

        comfort.

                        * *

        up

                    now

            taking chances

    with silence. More & more

            waiting

    for day   . . .   light

                        over the house.

He is counting: one   two

                                                    three   four
                              * *

When we rise

        the jungle

                                        Moves What that means

    grenades   come closer   white
                                                          lightning

            clears the range

                                                in the morning

        paper   hangs on   nothing

                        Nerve
                    * *

That makes some human cry

                            float

        like sunlight
                    * *

                                        But every night I sleep

                                                going

            to dawn like light.
                    * *

Here I live   my heart

            my family

        assemble.

Three counts.

* *

Sun

    clear

                Time

      my war

                          God

                    did it start.

One   Two   Three   Four.

      One

        Two

          Three

    &

    Sleep.

THINGS TO DO IN ANNE'S ROOM

Walk right in

    sit right down

        baby, let your hair hang down

    It's on my face that hair
    & I'm amazed to be here
    the sky outside is green the blue
    shows thru the trees

    I'm on my knees

       unlace Li'l Abner
      shoes
        place them under the bed
          light cigarette
       study out the dusty bookshelves,

                sweat

Now I'm going to do it

      SELF RELIANCE
      THE ARMED CRITIC
      MOBY DICK
      THE WORLD OF SEX
      THE PLANET OF THE APES

Now I'm going to do it

      deliberately

       take off clothes
      shirt goes on the chair
      pants go on the shirt
      socks next to shoes next to bed

the chair goes next to the bed

get into the bed
be alone
suffocate
don't die

    & it's that easy.

BLACK & WHITE MAGIC

for Anselm Hollo

1.

"Who's a 'black' artist?"

*

On this plane
w/ all the room in the world,

*

Dollars: 303 . . .

*

Secret Clouds

I can't get into you,
yet,

tho *Leaving Cheyenne*
was so beautiful:

it made me cry, perfectly
relaxed

a small gift I now am remembering
in Buffalo

*

2.

Breathe normally

Do not smoke

*

Awaiting rescue:

Eat, drink, sleep, or

Not . . . .

Don't.

*

You were stopped, & searched,
when least you expected.

What was found was *nothing.*

Don't expect it to be the same
coming back, baby.

*

Strapped: deprived

*

Shoot yourself: stay alive

*

3.

Ride it out

John F. Kennedy to Heathrow (London)
which involves you in

My Life With Jackie Kennedy

*

a human life

*

MAYA

Where civilization is taking place.

I mean, genuine civilization: no proportionate loss

of spleen.

"The head speaks out from the heart to the head connected

to the heart."

BABE RAINBOW

Light up

smoke

burn a few holes in the blanket

Burn a few holes in the Yellow blanket

burning

smoking

reading

TOUGH BROWN COAT

for Jim Carroll

Tough brown coat
Tie with red roses
Green cord vest

Brown stripes
on soft white
shirt

white T-shirt

White man,
   Tomorrow you die!

"You kidding me?"

ONE, LONDON

In Hyde Park Gate 14 white budgie scratchings mean
What? Black orchids on a wall serve for clouds, loom
Up from an orange bed floating, a host of words; Fall; heat coming on
White breathing disappearing as it defines this room

Above a friend his mate's asleep; he's somewhere else; England
Here clucks & poetry don't mix. October 1st; half-moon rising
Soon it seems to descend. Perhaps a clock is a good idea
It tells one what to do, when

Two weeks & a day past it seemed so easy to take, NY's room
& NY's speed made it seem easy, giving; easy living
Tho NY's room was someone else's, somewhere else too
Here words take their own sweet time arriving

Here to sleep a day & a night away seems mild. Still there's plenty to do;

Birds to be looked at, pills, a warm bath, letters to be written to you.

LAMENTS

So long, Jimi,

Janis, so long.

You both are great.

We love you.

But, O, my babies,

you did it wrong.

GOING TO CHICAGO

for Don Hall

Leaving first

On my way,

"Ave Atque Valium"

20 mgs.

& coffee

Thanks to the Air Hostess

dark eyes   dark hair

red lips
full

Red Nose in the air

*

A passing thought to John Sinclair

à la bas

Right On, John

*

We see you down there

from here

up in the air

it's the same air

as one breathes in

&

one breathes out . . .

"Down to you is Up"

. . . in between

here   and   there

&

here.

2.

The Prison Poems of Ho Chi Minh

Lunch Poems / In Memory Of My Feelings

Meditations In An Emergency

Advertisements For Myself

The Sweet Science

The Press

An American Dream

Mollie &
Other War Stories

Joe Liebling, Frank & Norman
ride with us
here.

3.

Change is in my pocket:

A John Kennedy American
half-dollar:

heads: Philip Whalen
tails: John Ashbery

(that's an old-master story)

flip it

it's in the air

The game is underway:
"Winning is my philosophy"

"Preparedness is the
only means toward Victory"

"Not Somehow
but
Triumphantly"

(that's the motto of The Salvation Army)

"There's a new day coming"

& if it's a nice day, we win

& if it's a stormy day,

can you dig it?

flying, under the weather

dig it

Fly Over

Fly Straight through

Fly big Baby, Fly!!

To The 2nd City.

Bye-bye.

In The Wheel

Winter,
1969

"Night-time ruffles the down
around your cheek"

IN MY ROOM

Green (grass)

    A white house   brown
                                  mailbox

       (Friendly pictures)

           *

TELEVISION   snow

                      (that's outside)

   No-mind

            No messages

     (Inside)

Thanksgiving   1969

TODAY IN ANN ARBOR

for Jayne Nodland

Today I woke up
   bright & early

Then.I went back to sleep

  I had a nice dream
 which left me weak
     so
  I woke up again
      dull, but still early.

  I drank some coke
    & took a pill

    It made me feel ill, but

   optimistic. So,

 I went to the Michigan Union for cigarettes

      *

I cashed a check today—
    but that was later. Now
  I bought cigarettes, &
      The Detroit Free Press.

 I decided to eat some vanilla wafers
   & drink coffee
     at my desk

   *

  There was no cream for
   the coffee. & the mail

wasn't out yet.

It pissed me off.

I drank some coffee, black
& it was horrible.

*

Life is horrible, &

I am stupid.

I think . . . . . . NOTHING.

Then I think, more coffee . . .
upstairs!

Jackie's face
picks me up.

She says,   "there's cream
upstairs"

Up more stairs vai the elevator:

cream   talk amiably to Bert
Hornback

*

Come downstairs
&
the mail has
come!
Lots
of mail!   I feel pretty good.

Together with my mail back in office.

Sitting.

                    *

Johnny Stanton says: "Ted,

          you are a myth in my heart."

          He is a myth in my heart!

     So, we are both myths!

                    *

Warmed by this, & coffee,

               I go on.   American Express
                              says:

                         "You owe us $1,906. Please

                              Pay *NOW*."

               I say, *sure!*

     ("Now" means "later")

                    *

Somebody else sends a postcard (Bill).

          He says,
                    "I am advertising your presence
                    at YALE, so please come!"

                         I say to Bill,

               "Have Faith, old

                    brother!   I'll be there
                         when you need me."

In fact, I say that to everyone.

That is the truth,

       & so,

         *

I open a beautiful letter

    from you. When we are both dead,

  that letter
        will be Part Two
               of this poem.

      *

But now we are both alive

    & terrific!

IN THE WHEEL

The pregnant waitress
asks
    "Would you like
some more coffee?"
Surprised out of the question
I wait   seconds   "Yes,
I think I would!" I hand her
    my empty cup, &
"thank you!" she says. My pleasure.

IT'S IMPORTANT

It's important not
to back out
of the mirror:

You will be great, but
You will be queer.

It's a complication.

DIAL-A-POEM

Inside
The homosexual sleeps
long past day break
We won't see him
awake
      this time around.

ANN ARBOR ELEGY

for Franny Winston d. sept 27th, 1969

Last night's congenial velvet sky
Conspired that Merrill, Jayne, Deke, you & I
Get it together at Mr. Flood's Party, where we got high
On gin, shots of scotch, tequila salt & beer
Talk a little, laugh a lot, & turn a friendly eye
On anything that's going down beneath Ann Arbor's sky
Now the night's been let to slip its way
Back toward a mild morning's gray
A cool and gentle rain is falling, cleaning along my way
To where Rice Krispies, English muffins, & coffee, black
Will make last night today. We count on that, each new day
Being a new day, as we read what the Ann Arbor News has to say.

SONG : PROSE & POETRY

to Alice Notley

My heart is confirmed in its pure Buddhahood

But a heavy list to starboard

                       makes me forget

From time to time.

             Breath makes a half turn

Downward & divides:

             it doesn't add up

2 plus 2 equals 1:   It's fun, yes,

But it isn't true, &

I can't love you

        this way.

2.

So, what'll I do, when you

              are far away

& I'm so blue?

        I'll wait.

            & I'll be true some day.

3.

That's all well & good. But

What happens in the mean time?

WAKE UP

Jim Dine's toothbrush eases two pills
activity under the clear blue sky; girl
for someone else in white walk by
it means sober up, kick the brunette out of bed
going out to earn your pay; it means out;
bells, ring; squirrel, serve a nut; daylight
fade; fly resting on your shoulder blades
for hours; you've been sleeping, taking it easy
neon doesn't like that; having come your way
giving you a free buzz, not to take your breath away
just tightening everything up a little; legs
pump; head, wobble; tongue, loll; fingers, jump;
drink; eat; flirt; sing; speak;
night time ruffles the down along your cheek

LIKE POEM

to Joan Fagin

Joan,
I like you
            plenty.

You'd do
            to ride the river with.

I take these tiny pills
to our love.

                Plenty.

Then I drink up the river.
Be seeing you.

PEACE

What to do
        when the days' heavy heart
                having risen, late
in the already darkening East
          & prepared at any moment, to sink
                        into the West
surprises suddenly,
        & settles, for a time,
                at a lovely place
where mellow light spreads
           evenly
             from face to face?

The days' usual aggressive
           contrary beat
               now softly dropped
into a regular pace
          the head riding gently its personal place
where pistons feel like legs
          on feelings met like lace.
                      Why,
take a walk, then,
          across this town. It's a pleasure
to meet one certain person you've been counting on
                    to take your measure
who will smile, & love you, sweetly, at your leisure.
                    And if
she turns your head around
          like any other man,
                go home
and make yourself a sandwich
          of toasted bread, & ham

                             with butter

lots of it
       & have a diet cola,
              & sit down
& write this,
       because you can.

SWEET VOCATIONS

After the first death there is plenty
Of Other but it's true
There is no other, too. One staggers
Weakly between the two. What fun is that?
It's no fun, that's what. After the first
Sniff, you notice the typewriter's been sharpened; you
Did it, so;

a, s, d, f, space . . . semi, l, k, j, space

Is it up & happy, this trip, like Merriweather Lewis
Whose California rides above the blue? or
Is it a down trip (John Keats)? I do love you:
"Down for you is up" when your head gets turned around

You look out the mirror at the self, & you preen,
You giggle because that it's so unlike you.

HALL OF MIRRORS

to Kristin Lewis

We miss something now
as we think about it
Let's see: eat, sleep & dream, read
A good book, by Robert Stone
Be alone

Knew of it first
in New York City. Couldn't find it
in Ann Arbor, though
I like it here
Had to go back to New York
Found it on the Upper West Side
there

I can't live with you
But you live
here in my heart
You keep me alive and alert
aware of something missing
going on

I woke up today just in time
to introduce a poet
then to hear him read his rhymes
so unlike mine   & not bad
as I'd thought another time

no breakfast, so no feeling fine.

Then I couldn't find the party, afterwards
then I did
then I talked with you.

Now it's back

& a good thing for us
It's letting us be wise, that's why
it's being left up in the air

You can see it, there
as you look, in your eyes

Now it's yours & now it's yours & mine.
We'll have another look, another time.

ANN ARBOR SONG

I won't be at this boring poetry reading
    again!
I'll never have to hear
    so many boring poems again!
& I'm sure I'll never read them again:
In fact, I haven't read them yet!

Anne won't call me here again,
To tell me that Jack is dead.
I'm glad you did, Anne, though
It made me be rude to friends.
I won't cry for Jack here again.

& Larry & Joan won't visit me here
    again.
Joan won't cook us beautiful dinners,
    orange & green & yellow & brown
    here again.
& Thom Gunn & Carol & Don & I won't get high
    with Larry & Joan here again
Though we may do so somewhere else again.

Harris & John & Merrill won't read
    in my class, again.
Maybe there'll never be such a class
    again:
I think there probably will, though
& I know Allen will follow me round the world
    with his terrible singing voice:
But it will never make us laugh here again.

You Can't Go Home Again is a terrific book:
I doubt if I'll ever read that again.
(I read it first in Tulsa, in 1958).
& I'll *never* go there again.

Where does one go from here? Because
I'll go somewhere again. I'll come somewhere again, too,
& You'll be there, & together we can have a good time.
Meanwhile, you'll find me right here, when you come through, again.

PEOPLE WHO DIED

Pat Dugan . . . . my grandfather . . . . throat cancer . . . . 1947.

Ed Berrigan . . . . my dad . . . . heart attack . . . . 1958.

Dickie Budlong . . . my best friend Brucie's big brother, when we were
                     five to eight . . . . killed in Korea, 1953.

Red O'Sullivan . . . hockey star & cross-country runner
                 who sat at my lunch table
                      in High School . . . car crash . . . 1954.

Jimmy "Wah" Tiernan . . . . my friend, in High School,
                 Football & Hockey All-State . . . car crash . . . 1959.

Cisco Houston . . . . . . died of cancer . . . . . . 1961.

Freddy Herko, dancer . . . jumped out of a Greenwhich Village
                                         window in 1963.

Anne Kepler . . . my girl . . . killed by smoke-poisoning while playing
                 the flute at the Yonkers Children's Hospital
                 during a fire set by a 16 year old arsonist . . . 1965.

Frank . . . . Frank O'Hara . . . . hit by a car on Fire Island, 1966.

Woody Guthrie . . . . dead of Huntington's Chorea in 1968.

Neal . . . Neal Cassady . . . died of exposure, sleeping all night
                 in the rain by the RR tracks of Mexico . . . 1969.

Franny Winston . . . just a girl . . . totalled her car on the Detroit-
                 Ann Arbor Freeway, returning
                 from the dentist . . . Sept. 1969.

Jack . . . Jack Kerouac . . . died of drink & angry sicknesses . . . in 1969.

My friends whose deaths have slowed my heart stay with me now.

TELEGRAM

to Jack Kerouac

Bye-Bye Jack.

See you soon.

A NEW OLD SONG

for Larry for Christmas

Head of lettuce, glass of chocolate milk

"I wonder if people talk about me, secretly?"

Guess I'll call up Bernadette today, & Dick

The Swedish Policeman in the next room, the Knife

Fighter. Why are my hands shaking? I usually think

Something like The Williamsburg Bridge watching the sun come

Up, wetly round my ears,

Hatless in the white & shining air. Throbbing

Aeroplanes zoom in at us from out there; redder

For what happens there.   Yes

It's a big world,

It has a band-aid on it, & under it

TRUE LOVE,

in a manner of speaking.

How We Live
In The Jungle
1969–1970

"Everything you are gone slightly mad.
America."

PEOPLE OF THE FUTURE

People of the future
while you are reading these poems, remember
you didn't write them,
I did.

FURTHER DEFINITIONS (WAFT)

(after Michael Brownstein)

a band of musicians: up tight

care not: like

understanding: dismissal

waiving: automatic pilot

compared to: no baloney

began to say: shut up

engraft feathers in a damaged wing: take a hike

experience to the full: kill

cultivators of land they do not own: friends

absolute: ready

pity: pull leg of

language here fails as mathematics has before it: at

is skilled in: oblivious

ended: borne

delicate constitutions: fascists

promoted: serf

one who dispenses with clothes: liar

lip to lip being the first, lip: right on

to heart, through the ear, is the second: "poof!"

graduate: push around

too clever riders are not good at horseplay: "Ma Femme"

food on a journey: chow

center of the earth: *hara*

the full moon: a friend to man

pineapples: heavy

having no wants, quite content: chatty

the power of slowly moving jaws: camp

exquisite: available night & day

critical, marking and epoch: straight

And Into Glory Peep: just for the hell of it.

SHAKING HANDS

for David Berrigan

This city night

    you walk in

no virgin   think of me

as I think of you

MARCH 17TH, 1970

Someone who loves me calls me

      & I just sit, listening

Someone who likes me wires me,

      to do something. I'll do it

Tomorrow.

Someone who wants to do me harm

      is after me

& finds me.

I need to kill someone.

      And that's what it's all about.

         Right Now.

SUNDAY MORNING

for Lou Reed

1.
It's A Fact

If you stroke a cat about 1,000,000 times, you will
generate enough electricity to light up the largest
American Flag in the world for about one minute.

2.
Turnabout

In former times people who committed adultery
         got stoned;
Nowadays it's just a crashing bringdown.

3.
A Mongolian Sausage

By definition: a long stocking: you fill it full of shit,
and then you punch holes in it. Then you swing it over
your head in circles until everybody goes home.

LADY

Nancy, Jimmy, Larry, Frank, & Berdie
George & Bill
        Dagwood Bumstead
                Donna, Joe, & Phil
Making shapes this place
           so rightly ours
                to fill
as we wish,
      & Andy's flowers too, do.
       *

      I've been sitting, looking
thinking sounds of pictures
         names
           of you

      *

    of how I smile now

      &

        Let It Be.

     *

& now I think to add
        "steel teeth"
                    "sucking cigarette"
   "A photograph of Bad."
        Everything you are gone slightly mad.
    America.

HOW WE LIVE IN THE JUNGLE

I am asleep
   next to The Hulk
warm behind,
     inside,
       all around me
Oranges,
    soft purples,
       greens, blue
Underneath & above
      wooden planks
        furniture,
Sky,
  big sky,
    all around the tree.
It's a house-tree.
     You feel at home here
        in the nut-bush.
First asleep
    next going into heat
      a stinging shower
& then,
   cooled, with a buzz on.

The Hulk is breathing easily now
       as her graceful form
moves purposefully into everyday life.
       The Hulk
often sleeps
    while I'm awake
      & vice-versa
& vice-versa.
    No matter.
      We live together in the jungle.

WIND

Every day when the sun comes up

The angels emerge from the rivers

Drily happy & all wet. Easy going

But hard to keep my place. Easy

On the avenue underneath my face.

Difficult alone trying to get true.

Difficult inside alone with you.

The rivers' blackness flowing just sits

Orange & reds blaze up inside the sky

I sit here & I've been thinking this

Red, blue, yellow, green, & white.

HEROIN

for Jim Carroll

(2) photographs of Anne

      80 years old

            lovely, as always

                    a child

          under an old fashion

                    duress

A Bibliography of Works
  by Jack Kerouac

          A white suit
           and a black dress
            w/high-necked
               mini-skirt

     strolling

    two by two

across   a   brown   paper   bag

      above   The Relation Ship

Warm white thighs   & floating bend   gia pronto

    my heart is filled with light

        al curry

  this

Life
that is
one, tho
the Lamps
be many   & proud   & there's a breeze sort of
                                          lightly moving the top
              of yr head

                    &   I'm going
                                   way over
                                   the white
                                          skyline

                          & I'll do
                    what I want to

              & you can't keep me here
                                   no-how

      & the streets are theirs now

                    & the tempo's

                          &   the space

LIFE IN THE FUTURE

for Donna Dennis

White powder

purple pill

pink pill

white powder

(2)

Blue air

white mist

blue / white sky

MARS

& it's Autumn in the Northern hemisphere

there.

THINGS TO DO ON SPEED

mind clicks into gear
& fingers clatter over the keyboard
as intricate insights stream

        out of your head:

        this goes on for ten hours:

    then, take a break: clean
    all desk drawers, arrange all
    pens & pencils in precise parallel patterns;
    stack all books with exactitude in one pile
    to coincide perfectly with the right angle
    of the desk's corner.

Whistle thru ten more hours of
arcane insights:

        drink a quart of ice-cold pepsi:
       clean the ice-box:

            pass out for ten solid hours

         interesting dreams.

       2.

Finish papers, wax floors, lose weight, write songs, sing songs, have
conference, sculpt, wake up & think more clearly. Clear up asthma.

treat your obesity, avoid mild depression, decongest, cure your
    narcolepsy,
treat your hyper-kinetic brain-damaged children. Open the
    Pandora's Box of amphetamine abuse.

3.

Stretch the emotional sine curve; follow euphoric peaks with descents
    into troughs
that are unbearable wells of despair & depression. Become a ravaged
    scarecrow.

Cock your emaciated body in
twisted postures   grind your caved-in jaw

          scratch your torn & pock-marked skin,
          keep talking, endlessly.

4.

Jump off a roof on the lower East Side

              or

            Write a 453-page unintelligible book

5.

Dismantle 12 radios

                string beads interminably

    empty your purse

                  sit curled in a chair
                    & draw intricate designs
                    in the corner of an envelope

6.

"I felt it rush almost instantly into
my head like a short circuit. My body

"I felt it rush almost instantly into
my head like a short circuit. My body
began to pulsate, & grew tiny antennae
all quivering in anticipation.

began to pulsate, & grew tiny antennae
all quivering in anticipation. I began
to receive telepathic communication from
the people around me. I felt elated."

7.

get pissed off.

Feel your tongue begin to shred,
lips to crack, the inside of the mouth
become eaten out. Itch all over. See
your fingernails flake off, hair & teeth
fall out.

Buy a Rolls-Royce

Become chief of the Mafia

Consider anti-matter.

8.

Notice that tiny bugs are crawling over your whole body
around, between and over your many new pimples.

Cut away pieces of bad flesh.

Discuss mother's promiscuity

Sense the presence of danger at the movies

Reveal

get tough

turn queer

9.

In the Winter, switch to heroin, so you won't catch pneumonia.

In the Spring, go back to speed.

Buffalo Days
Summer,
1970

"Dismantle twelve radios."

T E L E V I S I O N

for Larry Fagin

San Gabriel

Placer, Nevada. New York:

Buffalo. 24 Huntington, just off of Main.

$12.95 takes you

           where you want to go

quick; & quickly do you go.

$.30 will bring you back

sweating, worn out. Twice

as fast (as when you went) is

slow.

SOMETHING AMAZING JUST HAPPENED

for Jim Carroll, on his birthday

A lovely body gracefully is nodding
Out of a blue Buffalo
                 Monday morning
                             curls
softly rising color the air
                   it's yellow
above the black plane
                  beneath a red tensor

I've been dreaming. The telephone kept ringing & ringing
Clear & direct, purposeful yet pleasant, still taking pleasure
in bringing the good news, a young man in horn-rims' voice
                                   is speaking
while I listen. Mr. Berrigan, he says, & without waiting for an answer
    goes on,
I'm happy to be able to inform you that your request for
    a Guggenheim Foundation Grant
Has been favorably received by the committee, & approved. When
    would you like to leave?

Uh, not just yet, I said, uh, what exactly did I say with regards to
    leaving, in my application . . . I'm a little hazy at the moment.

Yes. Your project, as outlined in your application for a grant for the
    purpose
of giving Jim Carroll the best possible birthday present you could get
    him, through our Foundation, actually left the project, that is,
    how the monies
would be spent, up to us. You indicated, wisely, I think, that we knew
    more about what kind of project we would approve than you did,
    so we should

make one up for you, since all you wanted was money, to buy Jim a
   birthday gift.

Aha! I said. So, what's up?

We have arranged for you and Jim to spend a year in London, in a flat
   off of King's Row.
You will receive 250 pounds each a month expenses, all travel expenses
   paid, & a clothing allowance of 25 pounds each per month.
   During the year,
At your leisure, you might send us from time to time copies of your
   London works. By year's end I'm sure you each will have enough
   new poems for two books,
Which we would then publish in a deluxe boxed hardcover edition,
   for the rights to which we shall be prepared to pay a considerable
   sum, as is your due.
We feel that this inspired project will most surely result in The first
   major boxed set of works since Tom Sawyer & Huckleberry
   Finn! Innocents Abroad
in reverse, so to speak! We know your poems, yours & Jim's, will tell it
   like it is, & that is what we are desperate to know! So, when
   would you like to leave?
Immediately, I shouted! & Jim! I called, Jim! Happy Birthday! Wake
   up!

THINGS TO DO IN PROVIDENCE

Crash

Take Valium   Sleep

Dream &,

forget it.

*

Wake up new & strange

displaced,

at home.

Read The Providence Evening Bulletin

No one you knew

got married
had children
got divorced
died

got born

tho many familiar names flicker &
disappear.

*

Sit

watch TV

draw blanks

swallow

pepsi
meatballs

. . .

give yourself the needle:

"Shit! There's gotta be something
to do
here!"

*

JOURNEY   Seven young men on horses, leaving Texas.
TO SHILOH: They've got to do what's right! So, after
a long trip, they'll fight for the South in the War.
No war in Texas, but they've heard about it,
    & they want
to fight for their country. Have some adventures
    & make
their folks proud! Two hours later all are dead;
one by one they died, stupidly, & they never did
    find out why!
There were no niggers in South Texas! Only
    the leader,
with one arm shot off, survives to head back to Texas:
all his friends behind him, dead. What will happen?

*

Watching him, I cry big tears. His friends
were beautiful, with boyish American good manners,
cowboys!

*

Telephone New York: "hello!"

"Hello! I'm drunk! &
I have no clothes on!"

"My goodness," I say.

           "See you tomorrow."

*

Wide awake all night reading: *The Life of Turner*
       ("He first saw the light in Maiden Lane")
       A.C. Becker: Wholesale Jewels
             Catalogue 1912
       The Book of Marvels, 1934:
             The year I was born.

No mention of my birth in here.   Hmmm.

Saturday The Rabbi Stayed Home

(that way he got to solve the murder)

LIFE on the moon   by LIFE Magazine.

*

My mother wakes up, 4 a.m.: Someone to talk with!

Over coffee we chat, two grownups
I have two children, I'm an adult now, too.
Now we are two people talking who have known each other
             a long time,
Like Edwin & Rudy. Our talk is a great pleasure: my mother
a spunky woman. Her name was Peggy Dugan when she was young.
Now, 61 years old, she blushes to tell me I was conceived
before the wedding! "I've always been embarrassed about telling you
til now," she says. "I didn't know what you might think!"
"I think it's really sweet," I say. "It means I'm really
a love child." She too was conceived before her mother's wedding,
I know. We talk, daylight comes, & the Providence Morning Journal.
My mother leaves for work. I'm still here.

*

Put out the cat

                Take in the clothes
                   off of the line

     Take a walk,
         buy cigarettes

*

two teen-agers whistle
      as I walk up

          They say: "Only your hairdresser
              knows for sure!"

     Then they say,

      "ulp!"

     because I am closer to them.
They see I am not hippie kid, frail like Mick Jagger,
but some horrible 35 year old big guy!

        The neighborhood I live in is mine!

"How'd you like a broken head, kid?"
         I say fiercely.

     (but I am laughing & they are not one bit scared.)

     So, I go home.

     * * * *

Alice Clifford waits me. Soon she'll die
at the Greenwood Nursing Home; my mother's
mother, 79 years & 7 months old.

But first, a nap, til my mother comes home
from work, with the car.

*

The heart stops briefly when someone dies,
a quick pain as you hear the news, & someone passes
from your outside life to inside. Slowly the heart adjusts
to its new weight, & slowly everything continues, sanely.

*

Living's a pleasure:

I'd like to take the whole trip

despite the possible indignities of growing old,
moving, to die in poverty, among strangers:

that can't be helped.

*

So, everything, now
is just all right.   I'm with you.

No more last night.

*

Friday's great

10 o'clock morning sun is shining!

I can hear today's key sounds fading softly

& almost see opening sleep's epic novels.

TONIGHT

Winds in the stratosphere
Apologize to the malcontents
Downstairs

FAREWELL ADDRESS

Goodbye House, 24 Huntington, one block past Hertel
   on the downtown side of Main, second house on the left.
   Your good spirit kept me cool this summer, your ample space.
Goodbye house.

Goodbye our room, on the third floor. Your beds were much appre-
   ciated; we used them gratefully & well, me & Alice. & Alice's
   yellow blanket spread across the yellow slanted ceiling to make
   a lovely light, Buffalo mornings. There we talked, O did we ever!
Goodbye, our Third floor room.

& Goodbye other room across the hall. Typewriter music filled my
   heart Buffalo nights as I read on my bed while Alice wrote un-
   seen. Her Buffalo poems were terrific, & they were even about
   me! Some had you in them, too! So,
Goodbye room.

Goodbye second floor. Your bathroom's character one could grow to
   understand. I liked the sexy closed door of Chris's room, &
   light showing under the master's door at night; a good omen to me,
   always! Even your unused office offered us its ironing board, by
   moonlight.
You were friendly. Goodbye second floor of Richard's house.

Goodbye stairs. Alice knew you well.

& Goodbye first floor. Goodbye kitchen, you were a delight; you
   fed us morning, noon & night; I liked your weird yellow light, &
   your wall clock was out of sight! Meals we shared with Richard
   were gentle & polite; we liked them; we liked those times a lot.
Goodbye kitchen, you'll not be forgot.

& Goodbye Arboretum. (I mean TV room) Mornings, alone, I loved
    to sit in you, to read the news from the world of sports, as light
    poured into & through the house. Mornings were quiet pepsis.
    Nights I'd talk with Richard over beers. Good manners had some
    meaning here; I learned better ones with great delight. Goodbye
TV room. Thanks for your mornings and nights.

Goodbye vast dining hall, where we three & three dogs often ate
    of beef & drank red wine. Your table was long, & your chandelier
    a sight. Richard ate quickly, as did Alice, while I took my time,
    talking beneath your light. May we dine thusly many a night, days
To come. Goodbye dining room, & dogs who ate our bones with delight.

Goodbye Thelonius. Only Allen Ginsberg, for beauty, matches you. &
    Goodbye Ishmael. I liked your ghastly rough-house ways. You
    were the love/hate delight of Alice's days & nights. Many a fond
    lick you lolled her way, each of her trips. Goodbye Ishmael.
    Goodbye Oliver. You didn't say much, but you were always there,
    calling "Hey, wait for me!" like in those movies I used to like
    the best. When you three ate Bobby Dylan's SELF PORTRAIT, it
    put our friendship to the test. But it survived. & so,
Goodbye Ishmael, Thelonius, Oliver; friends, my brothers, dogs.

& Richard, goodbye, too, to you. You were the best of all our Buffalo
    life. Sharing with you made it *be* a life. We were at home in
    your house, because it's yours. It was a great pleasure, to come
    & go through your doors. Nothing gets lost, in anyone's life;
    I'm glad of that. We three had our summer, which will last. Poems
    last (like this one has); and so do memories. They last in poems,
    & in the people in them (who are us). So, although this morning
    under the sky, we go, Alice & I, you'll be flying with us as we fly.
    You come to visit, where we go, & we'll sometimes visit you in
Buffalo. Bring the dogs, too. & until then, our love to you, Richard.

Goodbye.

THREE SONNETS AND A CODA :
FOR TOM CLARK

1.

In The Early Morning Rain
To my family & friends   "Hello"
And money. With something inside us we float up
On this electric chair each breath nearer the last
Now is spinning
Seven thousand feet over / The American Midwest
Gus walked up under the arc light as far as the first person
the part that goes over the fence last
And down into a green forest ravine   near to "her"
Winds in the stratosphere
                         Apologize to the malcontents
Downstairs. The black bag & the wise man may be found
        in the brain-room.
what sky out there   Take it away
                  & it's off
one foot
           is expressing itself as continuum
the other, sock

2.

Tomorrow.   I need to kill
Blank mind part   Confusions of the cloth
White snow whirls everywhere.   Across the fields
in the sky the
              Soft, loose
stars swarm. Nature makes my teeth "to hurt"
shivering now   on 32nd Street   in my face & in my head
does Bobby Dylan ever come around here?   listen

it's alive   where exposed nerve jangles
& I   looming over Jap's American flag
In Public, In Private   The Sky Pilot In No Man's Land
The World Number 14   is tipsy as pinballs on the ocean
We are bored through . . . through . . . with our professionalism
Outside her
Windows

3.

I'm amazed to be here
A man who can do the average thing
                                                when everybody else is
going crazy   Lord I wonder just exactly what can happen
my heart is filled (filling)   with light
& there's a breeze   & I'm going
                                        way over
the white   skyline   do what I want to
Fuck it.
                        Tied up wit
Tie with red roses   The war of the Roses, &
War is shit.   White man, tomorrow you die!
Tomorrow means *now.*   "You kidding me?" now.
Light up   you will be great
It's a complication.   Thanksgiving, 1970, Fall.

CODA:

Being a new day my heart
is confirmed in its pure Buddhahood
activity under the clear blue sky
The front is hiding the rear (not)
which means we have (not) "protected ourselves"
by forgetting all we were dealt
I love all the nuts I've been in bed (with)

hope to go everywhere in good time
like, Africa: it would be tremendous (or not)
to drink up rivers. Be seeing you
to ride the river (with)   heads riding gently
its personal place   feet doing their stuff   up in the air
Where someone (J.) dies, so that we can be rude to friends
While you find me right here coming through again.

Winter In The Country
1970–1971

"There's a strange lady in my front yard."

Buddha On the

f·

"A little l·

She loca

The sa

am l·

Soli·

&

TO SOUTHAMPTON

Go
Get in Volkswagen
Ride to the Atlantic
Step out
See
Your shadows
On fog

At the second stop
The same ocean as
At the first

Back in Volkswagen
Ron's or somebody's
Backs up
Steps on the gas

COCA COLA 20 cents

Machine noise

Satisfaction

Home
Away from home.

CONVERSATION

"My name
"My name
"My name
is Wesley
is Wesley
is Wesley Jackson,
I am
I am
25 years
old,
I am 25 years old,
I am 25 years old,
and
my favorite
favorite
and my favorite
song
and my favorite
and my favorite song
and my favorite song
is *Valencia.*"

"Isn't
"Isn't that
beautiful,"
"Isn't that beautiful,"
Frank
Frank said.

"My name
"My name
"My name
is Wesley
Wesley
Jackson,
"My name is Wesley Jackson,
I am
I am
25 years
old,
I am 25 years old,
and
my favorite
my favorite
favorite
song
song
and my favorite song
my favorite song
is
Valencia."

"Isn't
that
beautiful,"
"Isn't that beautiful,"
Frank
said.

WISHES

Now I wish I were asleep, to see my dreams taking place

I wish I were more awake

I wish a sweet rush of tears to my eyes

Wish a nose like an eagle

I wish blue sky in the afternoon

Bigger windows, & a panorama—light, buildings & people in street air

Wish my teeth were white and sparkled

Wish my legs were not where they are—where they are

I wish the days warmly cool & clothes I like to be inside of

Wish I were walking around in Chelsea (NY) & it was 5:15 a.m., the .

     sun coming up, alone, you asleep at home

I wish red rage came easier

I wish death, but not just now

I wish I were driving alone across America in a gold Cadillac

     toward California, & my best friend

I wish I were in love, & you here

OPHELIA

ripped
out of her mind

a marvelous construction

thinking

no place; & you
not once properly handled

Ophelia

&

you can't handle yourself
feeling
no inclination
toward that
solitude,
love
by yourself

Ophelia

& feeling free   you drift

far more beautifully
than we

As one now understands

He never did see   you

you moving so   while talking flashed
& failed
to let you go

Ophelia

SCORPION, EAGLE & DOVE
A LOVE POEM

for Pat

November, dancing, or
Going to the store in the country,
Where green changes itself into LIFE,
MOVING ON, Jocky Shorts, Katzenmiaou
A Chesterfield King & the blue book
IN OLD SOUTHAMPTON,
                              you make my days special

You do Jimmy's, & Alice's,
Phoebe's, Linda's,
                    Lewis' & Joanne's, too . . .
& Kathy's (a friend who is new) . . .

& Gram's . . .
              who loved you,
                         like I do
          once . . .

& who surely does so since
                    that 4th of July last,
a Saturday,
          a day that left her free
to be with & love you
                    (& me)
                         (all of us)
just purely;
          clean;
               & selflessly;

                    *

     no thoughts

*

Just, It's true. As I would be
& as I am, to you
                    this
                        November.

TODAY'S NEWS

My body heavy with poverty (starch)
It uses up my sexual energy
      constantly, &
I feel constantly crowded

On the other hand, *One
Day In The Afternoon of
    The World*
Pervaded my life with a
    heavy grace
          today

I'll never smile again

Bad Teeth

But
I'm dancing with tears in my eyes
(I can't help myself!)   Tom
writes he loves Alice's sonnets,
    takes four, I'd love

to be more attentive to her, more
    here.
The situation having become intolerable
the only alternatives are:
    Murder & Suicide.

They are too dumb! So, one
becomes a goof. Raindrops
start falling on my roof. I say
Hooray! Then I say, I'm going out

At the drugstore I say, Gimme some pills!
    Charge 'em! They say
Sure. I say See you later.

Read the paper. Talk to Alice.
She laughs to hear
    Hokusai had 947 changes of address
In his life. Ha-ha. Plus everything
    else in the world
going on here.

Green TIDE; behind, pink against blue
Blue CHEER; an expectorant, *Moving On*
Gun in hand, shooting down
Anyone who comes to mind

IN OLD SOUTHAMPTON, blue, shooting up
THE SCRIPTURE OF THE GOLDEN ETERNITY
A new sharpness, peel apart to open, bloody water
& Alice is putting her panties on, taking off

A flowery dress for London's purple one
It seems to be getting longer, the robot
Keeps punching, opening up
A bit at a time. Up above

Spread atop the bed a red head sees
Two hands, one writing, one holding on.

LANDSCAPE WITH FIGURES
(SOUTHAMPTON)

There's a strange lady in my front yard
She's wearing blue slacks & a white car-coat
& "C'mon!" she's snarling at a little boy
He isn't old enough to snarl, so he's whining
On the string as first she & then he disappear
Into (or is it behind) the Rivers' garage.

                              That's 11 a.m.
In the country. "Everything is really golden,"
Alice, in bed, says. I look, & out the window, see
Three shades of green; & the sky, not so high,
So blue & white. "You're right, it really is!"

THREE POEMS : GOING TO CANADA

ITINERARY

Thursday & Friday:

(Southampton, New York City)

Wake up & crash land

pat the old lady

have a drink

tie shoes

take bus

change trains

go, to the doctor

score

HIGH

eat, beans &

bread pudding, get

slightly smashed on cheap red

take a walk

to clear your head

smoke hash / shoot smack

nod out / wake up with a start / take off

Go to Canada.

HOW TO GET TO CANADA

borrow 50 from George

Spend 2 for *Tarantula*

    and 4 for a little Horse

    and 5 for two meals

    and 1 or 2 for King-size Chesterfields

    and 2.50 to ride the bus

    and 2 more for taxicabs

    & 1 for tips & 25 cents for 1 more

    bus . . . . buy a ticket

    for 31. Check your bag, free.

    Steal *Night Song*, & *Prison Letters*

    From A Soledad Brother. Wait . . . . . . Fly:

    15 cents is plenty to keep you in the sky.

LOVE

Missing you

    in Air Canada

FRANK O'HARA

Winter in the country, Southampton, pale horse
as the soot rises, then settles, over the pictures
The birds that were singing this morning have shut up
I thought I saw a couple, kissing, but Larry said no
It's a strange bird. He should know. & I think now
"Grandmother divided by monkey equals outer space." Ron
put me in that picture. In another picture, a good-
looking poet is thinking it over; nevertheless, he will
never speak of that it. But, his face is open, his eyes
are clear, and, leaning lightly on an elbow, fist below
his ear, he will never be less than perfectly frank,
listening, completely interested in whatever there may
be to hear. Attentive to me alone here. Between friends,
nothing would seem stranger to me than true intimacy.
What seems genuine, truly real, is thinking of you, how
that makes me feel. You are dead. And you'll never
write again about the country, that's true.
But the people in the sky really love
to have dinner & to take a walk with you.

CRYSTAL

Be awake mornings. See light spread across the lawn
(snow) as the sky refuses to be any color, today
I like this boat-ride I'm being taken for, although
It never leaves the shore, this boat. Its fires burn
Like a pair of lovely legs. It's a garage that grew up
Sometimes I can't talk, my mouth too full of words, but
I have hands & other parts, to talk lots! Light the fire
Babble for you. I dream a green undersea man
Has been assigned to me, to keep me company, to smirk
At me when I am being foolish. A not unpleasant dream.
My secret doors open as the mail arrives. Fresh air
Pours in, around, before they close again. The winds are rushing
Up off of the ocean, up Little Plains Road. Catch the Wind
In my head, a quiet song. And, "Everything belongs to me
Because I am poor." Waiting in sexy silence, someone
Turns over in bed, & waiting is just a way of being with
Now a tiny fire flares out front the fireplace. Chesterfield
King lights up! Wood is crackling inside
Elephants' rush & roar. Refrigerator's gentle drone
Imagined footsteps moving towards my door. Sounds in dreams
In bed. You are all there is inside my head.

CLOWN

for Bill Berkson

There's a strange lady in my front yard
A girl naked in the shower, saying
"I'm keeping my boxes dry!" A naked artist
Smoking. Bad teeth. Wooden planks: furniture. Sky
One minute ago I stopped thought: 12 years of cops
In my life. & Alice is putting her panties on
Takes off a flowery dress for London's purple one
Out of the blue, a host of words, floating
March: awaiting rescue: smoke, or don't
Strapped: deprived. Shoot yourself: stay alive.
& you can't handle yourself, love, feeling
No inclination toward that solitude.
Take it easy, & as it comes. Coffee
Suss. Feel. Whine. *Shut up.* Exercise.
Turn. Turn around. Turn. *Kill dog.*
Today woke up bright & early, no mail, life
Is horrible, & I am stupid, & I think . . . Nothing.
"Have faith, old brother. You are a myth in my heart.
We are both alive. Today we may go to India."

CHINESE NIGHTINGALE

We are involved in a transpersonified state
Revolution, which is turning yourself around
I am asleep next to "The Hulk." "The Hulk" often sleeps
While I am awake & vice versa. Life is less than ideal
For a monkey in love with a nymphomaniac! God is fired!
Do I need the moon to remain free? To explode softly
In a halo of moon rays? Do I need to be
On my human feet, straight, talking, free
Will sleep cure the deaf-mute's heartbreak? Am I
In my own way, America? Rolling downhill, & away?
The door to the river is closed, my heart is breaking
Loose from sheer inertia. All I do is bumble. No
Matter. We live together in the jungle.

WRONG TRAIN

Here comes the man! He's talking a lot
I'm sitting, by myself. I've got
A ticket to ride. Outside is, "Out to Lunch."
It's no great pleasure, being on the make.
Well, who is? Or, well everyone is, tho.
"I'm laying there, & some guy comes up
& hits me with a billyclub!" A fat guy
Says. Shut up. & like that we cross a river
Into the Afterlife. Everything goes on as before
But never does any single experience make total use
Of you. You are always slightly ahead,
Slightly behind. It merely baffles, it doesn't hurt.
It's total pain & it breaks your heart
In a less than interesting way. Every day
Is payday. Never enough pay. A deja-vu
That lasts. It's no big thing, anyway.
A lukewarm greasy hamburger, ice-cold pepsi
          that hurts your teeth.

BUDDHA ON THE BOUNTY

for Merrill Gilfillan

"A little loving can solve a lot of things"
She locates two spatial equivalents in
The same time continuum. "You are lovely. I
am lame." "Now it's me." "If a man is in
Solitude, the world is translated, my world
& wings sprout from the shoulders of 'The Slave' "
Yeah. I like the fiery butterfly puzzles
Of this pilgrimage toward clarities
Of great mud intelligence & feeling.
"The Elephant is the wisest of all animals
The only one who remembers his former lives
& he remains motionless for long periods of time
Meditating thereon." I'm not here, now,
          & it is good, absence.

WINTER

The Moon is Yellow.

My Nose is Red.

Memorial Day
1971
Ted Berrigan
& Anne Waldman

"I dreamed you brought home a baby."
— Alice Notley

MEMORIAL DAY

Today:

Open   Opening   Opened:

*

The angels that surround me
die

they kiss death
& they die

they always die.

*

they speak to us
with sealed lips
information operating
at the speed of light

speak to us

O speak to us

in our tiny head

*

deep calling out to deep

*

we speak all the time
in the present tense at the speed of Life

dead heads operating

At the speed of light

Today:

& it's morning

Take my time this morning

& learn to kill

to take the will
from unknown places,

kill this stasis

*

let it down
let it down on me

*

I was asleep
in Ann Arbor

dreaming

in Southampton

beneath the summer sun of a green backyard

& up from a blue director's chair

I heard a dead brother say
into the air

"Girl for someone else in white walk by"

*

I was asleep in New York

dreaming in Southampton

& beneath the sun of the no sun sun up from my morning bed

I heard the dead, the city dead

The devils that surround us
never die

the New York City devil inside me
alive all the time

he say

"Tomorrow you die"

*

I woke up
as he typed that down:

"Girl for someone else in white walk by"

& then,

so did I.

So my thanks to you
the dead.

The people in the sky.

*

A minute of silent pool
for the dead.

*

& now I can hear my dead father saying,

"I stand corrected."

*

Dolphins, (as we speak)
are carrying on 2
conversations simultaneously

& within the clicks of one
lie the squeaks of the other

they are alive in their little wandering pool

*

"I wonder what the dead people are doing today?"

(taking a walk, 2nd St. to GEM SPA)

(or loping down Wall St.

Southampton)

*

ghost the little children

           ghost radio   ghost toast

         ghost stars

     ghost airport

        the ghost of Hamlet's father

ghost typewriter

       ghost lover

           ghost story

ghost snow   roasted ghost

    ghost in the mirror ghost

happy ghost   most ghost

*

I dreamt that Bette Davis was a nun, we
Were in a classroom, after school, collating
The World. Jr. High. A knocking at the door, I
went to answer (as Bette disappeared), & found my mother
Standing in the hallway.
               "Teddy," she said, "here
Is my real *mother,* who brought me up, I've always wanted
for you to meet her." Beside my mother stood

a tall, elegant lady, wearing black, an austere, stylish
Victorian lady whose eyes were clear & black; grand as
Stella Adler, but as regal & tough as Bette Davis.

Later that evening she sent me out for kippers for her bed-
time snack, giving me a shilling to spend. I went for them
to Venice, to a Coffee-House, which had a canal running right
        through it,
& there I ran into Ron, sitting with a beautiful boyish adolescent
blonde. "She's a *wonderful* lady," Ron said, & I was pleased.
Ron left shortly with the blonde nymphet, & I wondered a minute
about Pat (Ron's wife); but decided that Ron must know what he's
        doing. The girl, I thought, must be The Muse.

*

She is a muse

gone but not forgotten

*

50 STATES

state of grace

the milk state

Oregon

stateroom

state of anxiety

hazy state

estate

statement

Rugby Kissick state

Florida

the empire state

disaster state

the lightbulb state

soup state

Statue of Liberty

state of no return

the White Bear state

doped state

recoil state

Please state your name, address, occupation

the German shepherd state

bent on destruction

                state

the farmer state

state of no more parades

the tobacco state

statesman

stately

state prison

stasis

status

static

station wagon

State Flower

*

state of innocence

*

ambition state

North Carolina

Jasper's state

the united state

big state

state your cause

income state

jump the gun state

Roman nose state

manic depression state

hospital state

speed state

calculated state

gone forever state

the body state

the death body state

*

In New York State

in 'Winter in The Country'

at night you write

while someone

(Alice) sometimes sleeps & dreams;

awake she writes

22.

I dreamed you brought home a baby
Solid girl, could already walk
In blue corduroy overalls
Nice & strange, baby to keep close
I hadn't thought of it before
She & I waited for you out by the door
Of building, went in
Got you from painting
Blue & white watercolor swatches
We got on a bus, city bus
One row of seats lining it & poles
It went through the California desert
Blue bright desert day

In the country of old men I said

pretty good

& tho I live there

no more

"you can say that again."

Pretty good.

*

It takes your best shot,
                    to knock off whatever,

so, we take our best shots,
                              it gives us a boot or two

            we just do it

                    we wouldn't know what to tell you

        if our lives depended upon it!

                Anne?

            but Anne's already talking

across from me   across my life

            across the mailman's
        locked box,

                        over the mailman
                                I mean
            where a woman is alive
                            a mailman her friend
                    as you all know
            having met the man at the Met
        introduced by Vincent,
                        & loved by Joe:

        Joe's introductions go on,

the tongue, the ears burn   on Memorial Day

        at Anne's turn:

                *

Dear Mr. Postman:

Please take this from me

to me.

*

I'm delivered without a hitch
to myself

*

I'm a woman in the Prime of Strife

I speak for all you crazy ladies

past & present

& I say,

NO MESSAGES

*

Nothing can be helped.   Nothing gets lost.

*

Blink

the eye is closed

& I am asleep

blink

the eye is open

& I am awake

in the *real* wide-eye world   nothing gets lost

*

Today was a day to remember death:

I remember the death

of Hitler

& now I think of The Song of Roland

Roland's death

& now I think to see
if there were similarities

& I now I see there were . . .

*

& now I wonder what Tom Clark thinks

Edwin, Alex, Dick . . .

Mike?

*

A lung aching in the room

inside Mike

disease bringing you a little closer

Forget it!

Piss on it!

Kiss my ass!

he say

in his absolute way

Everybody obey

But

we are all victims

(me too)

& we all love life

(too bad)

*

I told Ron Padgett that I'd like to have

NICE TO SEE YOU

engraved on my tombstone.

Ron said he thought he'd like to have

OUT TO LUNCH

on his.

*

Dear Lewis:

I've been down but I'm surfacing

I've been lost but now I'm found

"One will leaf one's life all over again"

you say

& you are right

around & around & around go the swirling leaves

Death is *not* is *not* so horrible   today

*

The poison in the needle

floods my body

it hurts my head

it hurts my head

Poison from the needle
                    floods my bloodstream

                                        it detonates my head

                                        it detonates my head
I should put that needle down
                              but tomorrow I'll be dead.
                    *
    I recognized myself in a dream too, (Ted)

            we met & parted

                              Hello & Goodbye

                    simple as that

            my life recognized my death
Waiting on you
                              *
    The heart stops briefly when someone dies, one

    massive slow stroke as someone passes

        from your outside life to your inside,
                                        & then

                              everything continues

                                        sanely
                    *
        & I believe in you.
                    *
News of my cat

                    poor cat
                              descendant of Frank O'Hara's cat

he's dead

                              I grieve

              let it down

              let it down on me

                              *

X died, & Joe knew, but didn't want to have to tell anyone; but Carol
knew, & so, at Ken's 12th Night party she told me. After a few min-
utes, I took Martha home, & then I walked home myself, across town,
through Tompkins Square Park, to Avenue D & 2nd Street. I went to
bed, & then I started to cry; & I stayed in bed for three days, & cried,
& slept. And now I'm crying a little again. But then I got up, I said
"well, that's enough, fuck it!", & I got dressed, & went over to visit
Anne & Lewis as before.

                              *

      Bernadette had to arrange her mother's funeral age 15

              & we're in Rattner's   3 AM

      & she's telling me how her father died before that

      & all the death around her

                              surrounding her

              so many relatives

                      & how she just thought
                      that's what people do

                              "They die"

      & she was so good & obedient until her uncle died

      & then

                      something just snapped

Then she sent me this 2 days later:

Deaths, causes: tuberculosis, syphilis, dysentery, scarlet fever and streptococcal sore throat, diptheria, whooping cough, meningococcal infections, acute poliomyelitis, measles, malignant neoplasms, leukemia and aleukemia, benign neoplasms, asthma, diabetes, anemias, meningitis, cardiovascular-tenal diseases, narcolepsy, influenza and pneumonia, bronchitis, other broncho-pulmonix diseases, ulcer of stomach and duodenum, appendicitis, hernia and intestinal obstruction, gastritis, duodenitis, enteritis, and colitis, cirrhosis of liver, acute nephritis, infections of kidney, hyperplasis of prostrate, deliveries and complications of pregnancy, childbirth, and the puerperium, abortion, congenital malformations, birth injuries, postnatal asphyxia, infections of newborn, symptoms, senility, and ill-defined conditions, motor vehicle accidents, falls, burns, drowning, railroad accidents, firearms accidents, poison gases, other poisons, suicide, homicide.

*

I asked Joe Brainard
    if he had anything to say about death:

       & he said,
           "Well,
                 you always get
                 lots of flowers
                     when you die."

      Which is so true,
    especially for men. That is,
  it's *only* when you die that you get
      flowers,
             if you are a male

        I don't think
      I've *ever* been sent flowers

    Not even on Memorial Day.

I know I've never sent Joe any flowers.

Once I *took* a flower
from a nearby grave where there were
lots of them

it was in a little sharp-
pointed glass tube

& stuck the pointed end into the earth,
in front of Frank O'Hara's grave
so that the small-pink-flower
stood up.

On the gravestone it said:

GRACE TO BE BORN AND LIVE AS VARIOUSLY AS POSSIBLE

OK. I'll buy that.

& once I picked a different pink flower
from the earth
in front
of Guillaume Apollinaire's grave.

On his gravestone in French there was a poem in the shape of
a heart.

I had to go to the bathroom
so I left then

& went to a cafe
across from Pere Lachaise

They had a bathroom there   I had une pernod there

& then another

*

the shape of the American I am not

Still Life

                        the Chinese see nothing tragic in death
but for me the clue is you

the whistle of a bird or two
you are now dead
                        & I'm struck by how young

            we are
                        (were)

& how useless to speak

                    Let it down
                    Let it down on me

                        • • •

                                please

                        I love you

                        I'm sorry

                    • • •

            The evolution of man & society
            is not to be taken lightly   I advance
            upon the men   their quiet
            I'm certain   is fooling me . . .

                            *

I sat up late in a room in Manhattan
            & read about   the death
                            of Guillaume Apollinaire
                    dead in his bed
                            of pneumonia
                        after surviving shrapnel
                    in his head
                            in The World War

a young girl (Sandy) peacefully
sleeping in my bed

*

It is night. You are asleep. & beautiful tears
have blossomed in my eyes. Guillaume Apollinaire is dead.
The big green day today is singing to itself
A vast orange library of dreams, dreams
Dressed in newspaper, wan as pale thighs
Making vast apple strides towards "The Poems."
"The Poems" is not a dream. It is night. You
Are asleep. Vast orange libraries of dreams
Stir inside "The Poems." On the dirt-covered ground
Crystal tears drench the ground. Vast orange dreams
Are unclenched. It is night. Songs have blossomed
In the pale crystal library of tears. You
Are asleep. A lovely light is singing to itself,
In "The Poems," in my eyes, in the line, "Guillaume
            Apollinaire is dead."

*

A year or so later
            another poet told me that he really liked that poem.
First of all, he said,
            I can't tell any one of your sonnets
        from any other one,
                but this one I can.

*

I was afraid of that.
                Jim Brodey

*

Lonesome Train

• • •

Assassination Bizarre

• •

*

I'm the girl in the rain the girl on the street
the girl in the trance the girl at your feet the
girl who just got off the girl who plays the piano
the girl who fucks the girl in the red sweater the
girl in the airplane the girl in Mexico the girl
in the lake the girl from the Village the girl
in heaven the girl on the run the girl at the
bank the girl upstairs the girl in the photograph
the girl on the sofa the nervous girl
the girl under pressure the girl with the yellow
cup

*

I asked Tuli Kupferberg once, "Did you really jump off of

The Manahttan Bridge?" "Yeah," he said, "I really did." "How

come?" I said. "I thought that I had lost the ability to love,"

Tuli said. "So, I figured I might as well be dead. So, I went one

night to the top of The Manhattan Bridge, & after a few min-

utes, I jumped off." "That's amazing," I said. "Yeah," Tuli said,

"but nothing happened. I landed in the water, & I wasn't dead.

So I swam ashore, & went home, & took a bath, & went to

bed. Nobody even noticed."

*

If I could live it over, I wouldn't
but I wouldn't mind watching the movie

                    a big talkie

                              a big ghost

                    Get it while you can

                              *

the secret is this:

            Absolutely Without Regret

                        don't mess

                              back off

                                    steer clear

            but

                        I doan wanna hear anymore about
                                          that
I doan wanna hear any more about that

            I doan wanna hear any more about that

      I doan wanna hear any more about that

                  I doan wanna hear any more about that

                  I doan wanna hear any more about that

I doan wanna hear any more about you I doan wanna hear any more
                                          about you
                  I doan wanna hear any more about you

                  I doan wanna hear any more about you

            I doan wanna hear any more about you

                  I doan wanna hear any more about them

      I doan wanna hear any more about him

I don't wanna hear any more about President Nixon

(repeat)

There goes another geese on his way
to death
        blam blam

   b
    u
     c
      k
       s
        h
         o
         t

*

I tried my best to do my father's will

You don't want me baby got to have me any-how.

I tried my best to do my father's will

You don't want me baby got to have me any-how.

        Oh Lord,
            have mercy

        Oh Lord,
            have mercy

        Oh Lord,
            have mercy

     Have mercy,
        Lord.

＊

If it don't come across

FUCK IT

                                     & if your heart ain't in it,

ditto.

I met myself

       in a dream

                      Everything was just all right

Here comes two of you

       Which one will be true?

I'm beginning

       to see the light

                     How does it feel?

It feels,

       Out of sight!

＊

"The trumpets are coming from another station
and you do your best to tune them out"

says Mike

the wisest-assed guy I know.

"If my manner of song disturbs the dead the living
and the near dead it is because
near the dead end you can't dance"

—Andrei Codrescu

—312—

*

John Garfield William Saroyan Clarrise Rivers Harris Schiff
Ray Bremser Lewis MacAdams Tom Clark Bernadette

"Everybody's a hero.

Everybody makes you cry."

It makes you grin to say that

But you didn't say it

You dreamed it
in the after-life

I am not that man.

*

This February I dream when it's my turn to go to the moon (doom)
a little piece of string will be hanging outside
my window as I rise, arise

but I am not that woman

*

I am the man who couldn't kiss his mother

goodbye.

But I could leave.

& so I left.

& now, on visits, we kiss

Hello, Goodbye.

& I have no other thoughts about it, Memorial Day.

*

O you who are dead, we rant at the sky

no action

but pain in the heart
& a head that don't understand
the meaning of "heart" or "have heart"
or
"take heart"

She is walking away with herself

away from despair

she's that lucky girl!

graceful, &

complicated   head
(heart)

*

Who's keeping me alive

& what

I praise the lord for every day you & you & you & you & you

& you & you & you

Brothers & Sisters

You are with me on Sweet Remembrance Day.

*

& Now the book is closed

The windows are closed   The door is closed

          The house is closed

                              The bars are closed

The gas station is closed

                         The streets are closed

               The store is closed

          The car is closed

                         The rain is closed

          Red is closed

          & yellow is closed

          & green is closed

The bedroom is closed
               The desk is closed
                         The chair is closed

          The geraniums are closed

                    The triangle is closed

                         The orange is closed

     The shine is closed   The sheen is closed

          The light is closed

The cigar is closed
               The dime is closed

          The pepsi is closed

The airport is closed

The mailbox is closed

The fingernail is closed

The ankle is closed

The skeleton is closed

The melon is closed

The angel is closed   The football is closed

The coffee is closed   The grass is closed

The tree is closed

The sky is dark

The dark is closed

*

The bridge is closed

The movie is closed

The girl is closed   The gods are closed

The blue is closed

The white is closed

The sun is closed

The ship is closed

The army is closed

The war is closed

The poolcue is closed

Six is closed

eight is closed

four is closed

Seven is closed

The lab is closed   The bank is closed   The Times is closed

The leaf is closed
                The bear is closed
                                Lunch is closed

New York City is closed
                Texas is closed
                                New Orleans is closed

Miami is closed
                Okmulgee is closed
                                Sasebo is closed

Cranston is closed
                The Fenway is closed
                                Bellevue is closed

Columbia is closed
                9th Street is closed
                                2nd Street is closed

First Avenue is closed
                Horatio St. is closed
                                66 is closed

Painting is closed   Leibling is closed

Long Island is closed

Stones are closed   The afternoon is closed

Stones are closed   The afternoon is closed

The friends are closed
                    & Daddy is closed

                              & brother is closed & sister is
                                        closed

Your mother is closed
                    & I am closed—& I am closed

                                        & tears are closed

& the hole is closed   & the boat has left   & the day is closed.

                              —TED BERRIGAN & ANNE WALDMAN

Think of Anything
1971–1972

"waiting for my change."

REMEMBERED POEM

It is important to keep old hat
in secret closet.

OUT THE SECOND-FLOOR WINDOW

On St. Mark's Place

She walked

with the aggressive dignity

of those

for whom someone else's

irony

is the worst of disasters:

I loved her for it.

IN ANNE'S PLACE

It's just another April almost morning, St. Mark's Place
Harris & Alice are sleeping in beds; it's far too early
For a Scientific Massage, on St. Mark's Place, though it's
The *right* place if you feel so inclined. Later
Jim Carroll's double bums a camel from a ghost Aram Saroyan
Now, there goes Chuck, friend from out of a no longer existent past
Into the just barely existent future, wide-awake, purposeful
As Aram Saroyan's dad: a little bit more lovely writing, & then
Maybe a small bet on New York's chances this morning. It's not
Exactly love, nor is it faith, certainly it isn't hope; no
It's simply that one has a feeling, yes
You always do have a feeling & over the years it's become habit
Being moved by that; to be moved having a feeling,
So it's perfectly natural to get up & go to the telephone
To lay a little something down on your heart's choice
Calling right from where you are, in Anne's place,
As to your heart's delight, here comes sunlight.

POSTMARKED GRAND RAPIDS

Robert Creeley reading

Mark Twain and Mr. Clemens

STOPS
           while Philip Whalen
           writing
           "The Epic Airplane Notebook Poem"

Pauses . . .

     to discuss their drinking problem

with the Hostesses in the Sky

I'm watching
        writing
           drinking
               waiting for my change.

THINK OF ANYTHING

The Rose of Sharon
lights up
Grand Valley

Now
Robert Creeley speaks:

the air is getting
darker
and darker

the Rose of Sharon
moves

towards the door

and through.

TED BERRIGAN
& ROBERT CREELEY

MI CASA, SU CASA

for Lewis MacAdams

my crib your crib

the interior burns   I read

white palm over the coffee can

in the quiet

                a manual

of gentle but determined practices

"I want human to begin with"

A small voice walks across the grey empty room.

KIRSTEN

you're so funny! I'd give you

    all of my money, any-

time, just to see what you'd say!

    alas, all I have is a dime.

How you talk is my heart's

    delight. You are

more terrible than your step-dad,

    more great than bright light.

TOM CLARK

I take him
purely as treasure
His exquisite pain
pinpoints my evasive pleasure.

Don't think him to be
Any more than you see
& Don't be beastly
     to him. If you do
he'll let you see him
      seeing you:
& you'll wake up hating yourself
     for hating him.
You will.

THE COMPLETE PRELUDE

for Clark Coolidge

1.

Upon the river, point me out my course
That blows from the green fields and from the clouds
And from the sky: be nothing better
Than a wandering cloud
Come fast upon me
Such as were not made for me.
I cannot miss my way. I breathe again
That burthen of my own natural self
The heavy weight of many a weary day;
Coming from a house
Shall be my harbour; promises of human life
Are mine in prospect;
Now I am free, enfranchis'd and at large.
The earth is all before me, with a heart

2.

And the result was elevating thoughts
Among new objects simplified, arranged
And out of what had been, what was, the place
"O'er the blue firmament a radiant white,"
Was thronged with impregnations, like those wilds
That into music touch the passing wind;
Had been inspired, and walk'd about in dreams,
And, in Eclipse, my meditations turn'd
And unencroached upon, now, seemed brighter far,
Though fallen from bliss, a solitary, full of caverns, rocks
And audible seclusions: here also found an element
     that pleased her

Tried her strength; made it live. Here
Neither guilt, nor vice, nor misery forced upon my sight
Could overthrow my trust in Courage, Tenderness, & Grace.
In the tender scenes I most did take my delight.

3.

Thus strangely did I war against myself
What then remained in such Eclipse? What night?
The wizard instantaneously dissolves
Through all the habitations of past years
And those to come, and hence an emptiness;
& shall continue evermore to make
& shall perform to exalt and to refine
Inspired, celestial presence ever pure
From all the sources of her former strength.
Then I said: "and these were mine,
Not a deaf echo, merely, of thought,
But living sounds. Yea, even the visible universe was scann'd
And as by the simple waving of a wand
With something of a kindred spirit, fell
Beneath the domination of a taste, its animation & its deeper sway.

Easter Monday
1972–1977

"This mushroom walks in."

ELYSIUM

for Marion Farrier

It's impossible to look at it
Without the feeling as of
Being welcomed, say, to Paris
After a long boring train ride,

For women are like that:
They make one feel
he has travelled a long way
just being there.

And so well might he take
what comes, come
to what it is takes him.

BRIGADOON

for Bill Berkson

1.

"This mushroom walks in."

2.

"And one cannot go back except in time."

3.

"Nothing is gained by assurance as to what is insecure."

4.

"I have a machine-gun trained on Scotland Yard."

5.

"The body sends out self to repel non-self."

6.

"I can get close & still stay outside."

7.

"See the why, knowing what: the clear enigma."

8.

"a fragrant flowered shrub   blush   a clean tantrum."

CHICAGO MORNING

for Phillip Guston

Under a red face, black velvet shyness
Milking an emaciated gaffer. God lies down
Here. Rattling of a shot engine, heard
From the first row. The president of the United States
And the Director of the FBI stand over
A dead mule. "Yes, it is nice to hear the fountain
With the green trees around it, as well as
People who need me." Quote Lovers of speech unquote. It's a
    nice thought
& typical of a rat. And, it is far more elaborate
Than expected. And the thing is, we don't *need that* much money.
Sunday morning; blues, blacks, red & yellow wander
In the soup. Grey in the windows' frames. The angular
Explosion in the hips. A huge camel rests in a massive hand
Casts clouds a smoggish white out & up over the Loop, while
Two factories (bricks) & a fortress of an oven (kiln)
Rise, barely visible inside a grey metallic gust. "The Fop's Tunic."
She gets down, off of the table, breaking a few more plates.
Natives paint their insides crystal white here (rooms)
Outside is more bricks, off-white. Europe at Night.

NEWTOWN

Sunday morning: here we live jostling & tricky
blues, blacks, reds & yellows all are gray
in each window: the urbanites have muscles
in their butts & backs; shy, rough, compassionate
& good natured, "they have sex in their pockets"
To women in love with my flesh I speak.
All the Irish major statements & half the best
Low-slung stone. Upstairs is sleep. Downstairs
is heat. She seems exceedingly thin and transparent
Two suspicious characters in my head. They park & then
Start, the same way you get out of bed. The pansy is
Grouchy. The Ideal Family awaits distribution on
The Planet. Another sensation tugged at his heart
Which he could not yet identify,
half Rumanian deathbed diamond
Wildly singing in the mountains with cancer of the spine.

THE END

Despair farms a curse, slackness
In the sleep of animals, with mangled limbs
Dogs, frogs, game elephants, while
There's your new life, blasted with milk.
It's the last day of summer, it's the first
Day of fall: soot sits on Chicago like
A fat head's hat. The quick abounds. Turn
To the left, turn to the right. On Bear's Head
Two Malted Milk balls. "Through not taking himself
Quietly enough he strained his insides." He
Encourages criticism, but he never forgives it.
You who are the class in the sky, receive him
Into where you dwell. May he rest long and well.
God help him, he invented us, that is, a future
Open living beneath his spell. One goes not where
One came from. One sitting says, "I stand corrected."

THE GREEN SEA

Above his head clanged

Turning

And there were no dreams

               in this sleep.

Over this table.

METHOD ACTION

for Henry Kanabus

The frog sees the dog.   log?

             See the lamp?

  It is out.

        "Do you think I became
                 a dance-hall girl
           because
              I was *bad*?"

     It ain't gonna work.

         Because by morning
           it'll be gone.

The medicine I took
    to change
       the way I was.

        *

  And I'm the man who killed him.

A RELIGIOUS EXPERIENCE

I was looking at the words he
was saying . . . like . . . Okinawa . . .
bandage . . . real . . . form . . . and suddenly
I realized I had read somewhere that,
"in their language the word for 'idiot'
is also the word meaning 'to breathe through
your mouth.' " And I was simply left there,
in bed, *being looked at.*

LATE NOVEMBER

What said your light
you know, an answer refusing
I go to my store I maintain
animal inextricably between

illuminated, on the line
something lords in chair
all fixtured silvered
heart, your curtain, air

breathy air stirs white
knowing refusing running
Waitomo Cave New Zealand
couldn't catch the day, its curve, its more

Committed robbery with the Smothers Brothers
cops pursue us infinitely

OLD-FASHIONED AIR

to Lee Crabtree

I'm living in Battersea, July,
1973, not sleeping, reading
Jet noise throbs building fading
Into baby talking, no, "speechifying"
"Ah wob chuk sh'guh!" Glee.
There's a famous Power Station I can't see
Up the street. Across there is
Battersea Park
I walked across this morning toward
A truly gorgeous radiant flush;
Sun; fumes of the Battersea
Power Station; London Air;
I walked down long avenues with trees
That leant not ungracefully
Over the concrete walk. Wet green lawn
Opened spaciously
Out on either side of me. I saw
A great flock of geese taking their morning walk
Unhurriedly.
I didn't hurry either, Lee.
I stopped & watched them walk back up toward
& down into their lake,
Smoked a Senior Service on a bench
As they swam past me in a long dumb graceful cluttered line,
Then, taking my time, I found my way
Out of that park;
A Gate that was locked. I jumped the fence.
From there I picked up the *London Times,* came home,
Anselm awake in his bed, Alice
Sleeping in mine: I changed

A diaper, read a small poem I'd had
In mind, then thought to write this line:
"Now is Monday morning so, that's a garbage truck I hear,
    not bells" . . .
And we are back where we started from, Lee, you & me, alive & well!"

SOVIET SOUVENIR

What strikes the eye hurts, what one hears is a lie.
The river is flowing again between its banks.
Grant one more summer, O you Gods! that once I did not ask
The windows through which the bells toll are like doors

Because she is direct in her actions and in her feelings
Under the puns of the troop, there are frescoes
On the rudder, which you set against a bracelet's fire, and
Which goes toward you with each beat.

I find myself there; am I finally ill at ease with my own
Principle? Fortune be praised! Immense density, not divinely,
      bathes us
I hear walking in my legs
The savage eyes into wood look for the head they can live in

It's my window, even now, around me, full of darkness, dumb,
      so great!
My heart willingly again beginning crying out; and at the same time
      anxious, love, to contain.

PEKING

These are the very rich garments of the poor
Tousling gradations of rainbow, song & soothing tricks
With a crooked margin there & there is here: we
Are the waiting fragments of his sky, bouncing
      a red rubber ball in the veins.

Do you have a will? And one existing so forgets all
Desuetude desultory having to move again, take power from snow,
Evening out not more mild than beastly kind, into a symbol.
I hate that. I think the couple to be smiles over glasses, and

Questions not to find you, the which they have. O Marriage
Talking as you is like talking for a computer, needing to be
Abacus, adding machine, me. Up from the cave's belly, down from
      the airy populace
That lace my soul, a few tears from the last the sole surviving
      Texas Ranger,

Freed, freely merge with your air, dance. Blue are its snowflakes
Besprinkled blue lights on his eyes, & flakes. For her

I'd gladly let the snake wait under my back, and think, to walk,
And pass our long love's day. Landscape rushing away.

SCORPIO

If I don't love you I
Won't let it show. But I'll
Make it clear, by
Never letting you know.

& if I love you, I will
Love you true: insofar
As Love, itself,
Will do.

& while I live, I'll be
Whatever I am, whose
Constant, impure, fire
Is outwardly only a man.

SERVICE AT UPWEY

Over Belle Vue Road that silence said
To mean an angel is passing overhead.
Anselm's round head framed peering in the garden door
Four & ½ hours before, I didn't hear
The doorbell ring—7:30 a.m. Greenwich Summer Time—
Announcing the arrival
Of the celebrated Greek-American Poet
from Chicago: John Paul! Was that
An Alice or a Mabel who let him in?
First to visit us
In Wonderful Wivenhoe, where
Once smugglers ran amok, smuggling
What? and now Alice goes out
To shoppe.

*

"I have only one work, & I hardly know what it is!"

*

My baby throws my shoes through the door.

*

Baby-talk woke up the world, today
little Anselm,
        Alice, Mabel,
& John Paul.

*

& me writing it down here.

*

This page has ashes on it

BALTIC STANZAS

Less original than
penetrating
very often
illuminating

has taken us
300 years
to recover from
the disaster of

The White Mountain
O Manhattan!
O Saturday afternoons!
you were a room

& the room cried, "love!"
I was a stove, & you
in cement were a dove

Ah, well, thanks for the shoes, god
I wear them on my right feet
since that bright winter when
rapt in your colors, O heat!

how we lay long on your orange bed
sipping iced white wine, & not thinking
the blue sky changed blues while we were drinking
Next day god said, "Hitler has to get hit on the head."

FROM A LIST OF DELUSIONS
OF THE INSANE
(WHAT THEY ARE AFRAID OF)

That they are starving.
That their blood has turned to water.
That they give off a bad smell.
Being poor.
That they are in hell.
That they are the tools of another power.
That they have stolen something.
That they have committed an unpardonable sin.
Being unfit to live.
That evil chemicals have entered the air.
Being ill with a mysterious disease.
That they will not recover.
That their children are burning.

L . G . T . H .

Queen Victoria dove headfirst into the swimming pool, which was
    filled with blue milk.
I used to be baboons, but now I am person.
I used to be secretary to an eminent brain surgeon, but now I am
    quite ordinary. Oops! I've spilled the beans!
I wish mountains could be more appealing to the eye.
I wash sometimes. Meanwhile
Two-ton Tony Galento began to rub beef gravy over his entire body.
I wish you were more here.
I used to be Millicent, but now I am Franny.
I used to be a bowl of black China tea, but now I am walking back
    to the green fields of the People's Republic.
Herman Melville is elbowing his way through the stringbeans
    toward us.
Oscar Levant handed the blue pill to Oscar Wilde during the fish
    course. Then he slapped him.
I used to be blue, but now I am pretty. I wish broken bad person.
I wish not to see you tonight.
I wish to exchange this chemistry set for a goldfish please.
I used to be a little fairy, but now I am President of The United States.

EASTER MONDAY

"Antlers have grown out the top of my shaggy head."

"And his conclusions to be unaccompanied by any opinions . . . ."

"You can't have two insides having an affair."

"Why not then spiritualize one's midday food with a little liquor?"

"The question seems prosecutorial." "The house is lost

In the room." "Loyalty is hard to explain."

"Hard fight gets no reward." "A woman has a spirit of her own."

"A man's spirit is built upon experience & rage." —Max Jacob.

In the air, in the house, in the night, bear with me

"I always chat to the golden partner."

"I'm working out the structures of men that don't exist yet."

"A gladness as remote from ecstasy as it is from fear."

"To go on telling the story."

"Give not that which is holy to dog."

IN BLOOD

"Old gods work"

"I gather up my tics & tilts, my stutters & imaginaries into the "up" leg

In this can-can . . ." "Are you my philosophy

If I love you which I do . . . ?" "I want to know

It sensationally like the truth;" "I see in waves

Through you past me;" "But now I stop—" "I can love

What's for wear:" "But I dredge what I've bottomlessly canned

When I can't tell you . . ." "I love natural

Coffee beautifully . . ." "I'm conjugally love

Loose & tight in the same working" "I make myself

Feature by feature" "The angel from which each thing is most itself,

   from each, each,"

"I know there's a faithful anonymous performance"

"I wish never to abandon you" "I me room he" To

"Burn! this is not negligible, being poetic, & not feeble."

SO GOING AROUND CITIES

to Doug & Jan Oliver

"I order you to operate. I was not made to suffer."
Probing for old wills, and friendships, for to free
to New York City, to be in History, New York City being
History at that time." "And I traded my nights
for Intensity; & I barter my right to Gold; & I'd traded
my eyes much earlier, when I was circa say seven years old
for ears to hear Who was speaking, & just exactly who
was being told . . . ." & I'm glad
      I hear your words so clearly
      & I would not have done it
         differently
      & I'm amused at such simplicity, even so,
inside each & every door. And now I'm with you, instantly,
& I'll see you tomorrow night, and I see you constantly, hopefully
though one or the other of us is often, to the body-mind's own self
more or less out of sight! Taking walks down any street, High
Street, Main Street, walk past my doors! Newtown; Nymph Rd
    (on the Mesa); Waveland
Meeting House Lane, in old Southampton; or BelleVue Road
    in England, etcetera
Other roads; Manhattan; see them there where open or shut up behind
    "I've traded sweet times for answers . . ."
"They don't serve me anymore." They still serve me on the floor.
    Or,
as now, as floor. Now we look out the windows, go in &
    out the doors.
(That front door which was but & then at that time My door).
    I closed it
On the wooing of Helen. "And so we left schools for her." For
She is not one bit fiction; & she is easy to see;
      & she leaves me small room

For contradiction. And she is not alone; & she is not one bit
lonely in the large high room &
invention is just vanity, which is plain. She
is the heart's own body, the body's own mind in itself
self-contained.
& she talks like you; & she has created truly not single-handedly
Our tragic thing, America. And though I would be I am not afraid
of her, & you also not. You, yourself, I,
Me, myself, me. And no, we certainly have not pulled down
our vanity: but
We wear it lightly here,
here where I traded evenly,
& even gladly
health, for sanity; here
where we live day-by-day
on the same spot.
My English friends, whom I love & miss, we talk to ourselves here,
& we two
rarely fail to remember, although we write seldom, & so must seem
gone forever.
In the stained sky over this morning the clouds seem about to burst.
What is being remembering
Is how we are, together. Like you we are always bothered, except
by the worst; & we are living
as with you we also were
fired, only, mostly, by changes in the weather. For Oh dear hearts,
When precious baby blows her fuse / it's just our way
of keeping amused.
That we offer of & as excuse. Here's to you. All the very best.
What's your pleasure? Cheers.

COMMUNISM

Red Air

& I can hear the red bus
                    sing
            Morning has broken
        meticulously

labelled   the East Wing is fossils

        sinister habits   antiques

in fact a pleasant park
                                a government department

                    bulbs

                    birth

            severe abundance swirlings

The most
spectacular object
in it

            a great
            shining
            prolific
            automatic
            electric
            churchyard
            map-maker

                            mute

                        flickering

                        imagination

   bejewelled

                                             coarse
                                            display

the euphonious person
  in hey-day
    wholesomeness
      taken

                                  over-large
                                     fuses

              With a little lantern above

              A sort of canopy

              pitched within a room

                                  architecture

Church
                with the exception of

              One steel office building

              A cold violent backside to you

A little saucer dome
                  imp anonymity
               little plateaus in various arms

            Swallower of former designs

                 true stone fan virile shadow

        functional sinews of mood & tempo of
              ballcourt

                    COFFEE

Square bracketing vision bubble dome

Central Presences Naked in the Shroud:

Sensible in the air

bronze pedestrian tree-ape

grace-note

the dizzying staircase

non-euphonious personal
disguise.

QUARTER TO THREE

"who is not here
causes us to drift"

wake up, throat dry,
that way, perpetually,

"and why deprived unless
you feel that you ought to be?" and

"Clarity is immobile." And, "We are hungry
for devices to keep the baby happy . . ."

She writes, "My hunger creates a food
that everybody needs."

"I can't live without you, no
matter who you are." "I think."

I write this in cold blood,
    enjoy.

A MEETING AT THE BRIDGE

He was one of the last of the Western Bandits.

"A fellow like you gets into scrapes.

"Gets Life. Spends most of it in jail.

"You gotta make a stand somewhere."

I guess. "You smell of disinfectant."

I guess. "Your kind

Drift from nowhere to nowhere, until

They get close. No telling

What they do then." Yeah, I guess that's just about right.

Do you fish? "No, I just go down and look at the water.

Pretty, ain't it?" Is it? No, it ain't.

It ain't pretty. It's

A carnival. A pig-sty. A regular

Loop-de-loop . . . . (spits) "I need some shoes."

" I REMEMBER "

I remember painting "I HATE TED BERRIGAN" in big black letters
    all over my white wall.

I remember bright orange light coming into rooms in the late
    afternoon. Horizontally.

I remember when I lived in Boston reading all of Dostoyevsky's
    novels one right after the other.

I remember the way a baby's hand has of folding itself around
    your finger, as tho forever.

I remember a giant gold man, taller than most buildings, at
    "The Tulsa Oil Show."

I remember in Boston a portrait of Isabella Gardner by Whistler.

I remember wood carvings of funny doctors.

I remember opening jars that nobody else could open.

I remember wondering why anyone would want to be a doctor. And
    I still do.

I remember Christmas card wastebaskets.

I remember not understanding why Cinderella didn't just pack up and
    leave, if things were all *that* bad. I remember "Korea."

I remember one brick wall and three white walls.

I remember one very hot summer day I put ice cubes in my aquarium
    and all the fish died.

I remember how heavy the cornbread was. And it still is.

A NOTE FROM YANG-KUAN

You stay in the Mental Institute of your life.
God sees dog—in the mirror. In this city
Below the river, my private life is of no interest,
Though allowed. For example, it would be nicer to kiss than
     to shoot up.
Visual indifference is a growth. Used. Was used. Useful.
A new way of appreciating has arrived. I
Should be a ride at Disneyland. People
Have basically split. And, the heart flutters.
Stunned, the metrics & melody of
The multiplication tables, I am a father, watching,
The poor, her broad thoughts, this local lifetime.
Here I shall be with it but never of it.
Being nothing in front of no-one again.

WORK POSTURES

The rain comes and falls.
A host of assorted artillery come up out of the lake.
The man who knows everything is a fool.
In front of him is his head. Behind him, men.

Few listeners get close. And
"Love must turn to power or it die."
This is a terrible present.
"Is this any way to run a Railroad?"

Flashing back 7 years I hear, "you will never go
any place for the second time again."
It's hard to fight, when your body is not with you.
& it's equally hard not to.

There is the dread that mind & body are one.
The cruelty of fear & misery works here.

FROM THE HOUSE JOURNAL

1.

I belong here, I was born
To breathe in dust
I came to you
I cannot remember anything of then
                    up there among the lettuce plots

I cough a lot, so I stay awake
I cannot possibly think of you
I get a cinder in my eye because
I hate the revolutionary vision of

"I have a terrible age," & I part
I have no kindness left
I do have the lame dog with me & the cloud
I kiss your cup, but I know so much.

I must have leisure for leisure bears
I to you and you to me the endless oceans of

2.

Now it next to my flesh, & I don't mean dust
I am sober and industrious
I see you standing in clear light
I see a life of civil happiness
I see now tigers by the sea,
                              the withering weathers of
I stagger out of bed
I stumble over furniture I fall into a gloomy hammock
I'm having a real day of it
I'm not sure there's a cure
You are so serious, as if you are someone
Yet a tragic instance may be immanent
Yes it's sickening that yes it's true, and
Yes it's disgusting that yes if it's necessary, I'll do it.

WHITMAN IN BLACK

For my sins I live in the city of New York
Whitman's city lived in in Melville's senses, urban inferno
Where love can stay for only a minute
Then has to go, to get some work done
Here the detective and the small-time criminal are one
& tho the cases get solved the machine continues to run
Big Town will wear you down
But it's only here you can turn around 360 degrees
And everything is clear from here at the center
To every point along the circle of horizon
Here you can see for miles & miles & miles
Be born again daily, die nightly for a change of style
Hear clearly here; see with affection; bleakly cultivate compassion
Whitman's walk unchanged after its fashion.

SOUTHWEST

We think by feeling and so we ride together
The child who has fallen in love with maps & charts,
The last, the sole surviving Texas Ranger, cajoling
Scheming, scolding, the cleverest of them all. What is there to know?

Questions. The very rich garments of the poor.
The very rack & crucifix of weather, winter's wild silence
In red weather. A too resilient mind. The snake
Waiting under each back. Not to forget to mention the chief thing:

Underneath a new old sign, a far too resilient mind;
And the heavy not which you were bringing back alone,
Cycling across an Africa of green & white, but to be a part
Of the treetops & the blueness, with a bark that will not bite.

The fields breathe sweet, as one of you sleeps while the other is fuming
    with rage.
Is he too ill for pills? Am I gonna ride that little black train
    one year from tonight?

TO HIMSELF

Now you can rest forever
Tired heart. The final deceit is gone,
Even though I thought it eternal. It's gone.
I know all about the sweet deception,
But not only the hope, even the desire is gone.
Be still forever. You've done enough
Beating. Your movements are really
Worth nothing, nor is the world
Worth a sigh. Life is bitterness
And boredom; and that's all. The world's a mudhole.
It's about time you shut up. Give it all up
For the last time. To our kind fate gives
Only that we die. It's time you showed your contempt for
Nature and that cruel force which from hiding
Dictates our universal hurt
In the ceaseless vanity of every act.

—LEOPARDI

(trans. by Ted Berrigan, Gordon Brotherston & George Schneeman)

REVERY

Up inside the walls of air listen
A sound of footsteps in the spaces out there
In the frightening purple weather
And hazy lights whose color night decomposes.

Late at night, rise up carcass and walk;
Head hanging, let somebody tell the story.
Maybe the machine under the palms will start up.
For one who waits

Under the arch of clouds, with familiar face,
Heart beating all out of proportion,
Eyes barely open, ears long since awake to what's coming:
It is very possibly Autumn, returning,

Leaving no footprints, leaving danger behind.
The head being out of line has fallen. I still want
      everything that's mine.

UNDER THE SOUTHERN CROSS

for Dick Gallup

Peeling rubber all the way up
SECOND AVENUE into Harlem Heights
Our yellow Triumph took us out of Manhattan tenement hells

Into the deer-ridden black earth dairylands.
Corn-fed murderers, COPS, waved us past
Low-slung Frank Lloyd Wright basements. We missed most deer.

You left me in Detroit, for money. In Freeport, Maine, our host
Shotgunned his wife into cold death, who was warm. Fuck him. Scoot
Ferried us to Portland, then leaped out of his life from atop the
        UN Building.

Enplaning next to the flatlands, we rubber-stamped our own passports
And in one year changed the face of American Poetry. Hepatitis
        felled you
Then on the very steps where the Peace Corps first reared its no-head.

Though it helped pass the long weekends, polygamy unsettled me
        considerably
In Ann Arbor, where each day's mail meant one more lover dead.
        My favorite
Elm tree died there as well. But Europe beckoned, and we went, first

Pausing to don the habits of Buffalo, in Buffalo. After that it was
        weak pins
& strong needles, but travel truly does broaden. It broadened us,
And we grew fat & famous, or at least I did. You fell

For a Lady from Baltimore near the Arno. Then you fell
Into the Arno. You drowned & kept on drowning; while I, in my
Silver threads, toured the Historical Tate, & mutilated

& strong needles, but travel truly does broaden. It broadened us,
And we grew fat & famous, or at least I did. You fell

For a Lady from Baltimore near the Arno. Then you fell
Into the Arno. You drowned & kept on drowning; while I, in my
Silver threads, toured the Historical Tate, mutilated

A well-thought of Blake while England slept.
In Liverpool a Liverpudlian dropped his bottle of milk beneath a
    neon light,
Smashing it to smithereens. The sidewalk white with milk made us cry.

And so we left. Back in the USA, on crutches, we acquired ourselves
    a wife
For 12 goats and a matched pair of Arabian thoroughbreds picked up
    on a whim
From a rug-peddlar in Turkestan. God knows what we gave to him.

Now I'm living in New York City once again, gone grey, and mostly
    stay in bed
While you are pacing your floor in Baltimore. But we aren't "black"
    yet, not
By a long shot. Oh No! This trip doesn't end

Until we drop off our yellow Triumph somewhere still far away
From where we are now. No, this ain't it yet.
There's black coffee & glazed donuts still due us, bubba,

At a place called The Jesse James Cafe. So, hit it. Let's burn rubber.
TIMES CRITIC DESPISES CURRENT PLAY, a Post reports.
Dangling from it, in the wind, his body gently sways.

Come on, floor this Mother! Whoops! Don't hit that lonely old
    grubber.

Not Dying
1977–1979

"No joke!"

ALLEN GINSBERG'S "SHINING CITY"

for Alice

But that dream . . . oh, hell!
maybe, like Jack, just drink muscatel!
But that won't work. A "Pharmacia"
is where you get your pills. "Shining
City." & in its space & time one can find
a "Position inferior to Language." & occupy
beautiful, discrete, & almost ordinary
Places. —But that won't work . . .
. . . that dream . . . "oh, Hell!"

IN THE 51ST STATE

for Kate

The life I have led
being an easy one
has made suicide
impossible, no?

Everything arrived
in fairly good time;
women, rolls, medicine
crime—poor health

like health
has been an inspiration.

When all else fails I read the magazines.

Criticism like a trombone used as a gate
satisfies some hinges, but not me.
I like artists who rub their trumpets with maps
to clean them, the trumpets or the maps.

I personally took
33 years to discover
that blowing your nose is necessary sometimes
even tho it is terrifying. (not aesthetic).

I'd still rather brindle.

I wasn't born in this town
but my son, not the one born in Chicago,
not the one born in England, not
the one born in New England, in fact, my daughter
was. She looks like her brother by another mother
and like my brother, too.

Her forehead shines like the sun
above freckles and I had mine
and I have more left.

I read only the books you find in libraries or drugstores
or at Marion's. Harris loans me Paul Pines'
to break into poetry briefly.

Au revoir.
            (I wouldn't translate that
as "Goodbye" if I were you.)

A woman rolls under the wheels in a book.
Here they are the wheels, so I hear.

Bon voyage, little ones.

Follow me down
Through the locks. There is no key.

RED SHIFT

Here I am at 8:08 p.m. indefinable ample rhythmic frame
The air is biting, February, fierce arabesques
    on the way to tree in winter streetscape
I drink some American poison liquid air which bubbles
    and smoke to have character and to lean
In. The streets look for Allen, Frank, or me, Allen
    is a movie, Frank disappearing in the air, it's
Heavy with that lightness, heavy on me, I heave
    through it, them, as
The Calvados is being sipped on Long Island now
    twenty years almost ago, and the man smoking
Is looking at the smilingly attentive woman, & telling.
Who would have thought that I'd be here, nothing
    wrapped up, nothing buried, everything
Love, children, hundreds of them, money, marriage-
    ethics, a politics of grace,
Up in the air, swirling, burning even or still, now
    more than ever before?
Not that practically a boy, serious in corduroy car coat
    eyes penetrating the winter twilight at 6th
& Bowery in 1961. Not that pretty girl, nineteen, who was
    going to have to go, careening into middle-age so,
To burn, & to burn more fiercely than even she could imagine
    so to go. Not that painter who from very first meeting
I would never & never will leave alone until we both vanish
    into the thin air we signed up for & so demanded
To breathe & who will never leave me, not for sex, nor politics
    nor even for stupid permanent estrangement which is
Only our human lot & means nothing. No, not him.
There's a song, "California Dreaming", but no, I won't do that.
I am 43. When will I die? I will never die, I will live

To be 110, & I will never go away, & you will never escape from me
    who am always & only a ghost, despite this frame, Spirit
Who lives only to nag.
I'm only pronouns, & I am all of them, & I didn't ask for this
    You did
I came into your life to change it & it did so & now nothing
    will ever change
That, and that's that.
Alone & crowded, unhappy fate, nevertheless
    I slip softly into the air
The world's furious song flows through my costume.

AROUND THE FIRE

What I'm trying to say is that if an experience is
proposed to me—I don't have any particular interest
in it—Any more than anything else. I'm interested in
anything. Like I could walk out the door right now and go some-
where else. I don't have any center in that sense. If you'll look
in my palm you'll see that my heart and my head line are
the same and if you'll look in your palm you'll see that it's
different. My heart and my head feel exactly the same. Me,
I like to lay around of a Sunday and drink beer. I don't feel
a necessity for being a mature person in this world. I mean
all the grown-ups in this world, they're just playing house, all
poets know that. How does your head feel? How I feel is
what I think. I look at you today, & I expect you to look
the same tomorrow. If you're having a nervous breakdown, I'm
not going to be looking at you like you're going to die, because
I don't think you are. If you're a woman you put yourself
somewhere near the beginning and then there's this other place
you put yourself in terms of everybody. "The great cosmetic strange-
ness of the normal deep person." Okay. Those were those people—and
I kept telling myself, I have to be here, because I don't have
a country. How tight is the string? And what is on this particular
segment of it? And the photographer, being black, and the writer,
me, being white, fell out at this point. And he didn't want to
look at it—I mean it's nothing, just some drunk Indians riding
Jersey milk cows—but I wanted to see it, I mean it was right
in front of my eyes and I wanted therefore to look at it.
And death is not any great thing, it's there or it's not. I mean
God is the progenitor of religious impetuosity in the human beast.
And Davy Crockett is right on that—I mean he's gonna shoot a bear,

but he's not gonna shoot a train, because the train is gonna run right over him. You can't shoot the train. And I always thought there was another way to do that. And it is necessary to do that and we bear witness that it is necessary to do it. The only distinction between men and women is five million shits.

CRANSTON NEAR THE CITY LINE

One clear glass slipper; a slender blue single-rose vase;
one chipped glass Scottie; an eggshell teacup & saucer, tiny,
fragile, but with sturdy handle; a gazelle? the lightest pink flowers
on the teacup, a gold circle, a line really on the saucer; gold
line curving down the handle; glass doors on the cabinet which sat
on the floor & was not too much taller than I; lace doilies? on
the shelves; me serious on the floor, no brother, shiny floor or
shining floor between the flat maroon rug & the glass doors of
     the cabinet:

I never told anyone what I knew. Which was that it wasn't
for anyone else what it was for me.

The piano was black. My eyes were brown. I had rosy
cheeks, every sonofabitch in the world said. I never saw them.

My father came cutting around the corner of the A&P
& diagonally across the lot in a beeline toward our front sidewalk
& the front porch (& the downstairs door); and I could see him, his
long legs, quick steps, nervous, purposeful, coming & passing, combing
his hair, one two three quick wrist flicks that meant "worrying" &
     "quickly!"

There were lilacs in the back yard, & dandelions in the lot.
There was a fence.

Pat Dugan used to swing through that lot, on Saturdays, not too tall,
in his brown suit or blue one, white shirt, no tie, soft brown men's
slippers on his feet, & Grampa! I'd yell & run to meet him &
"Hi! Grampa," I'd say & he'd swing my arm and be singing his funny
     song:

*

"She told me that she loved me, but

    that was yesterday. She told me

that she loved me, & then

    she went away!"

*

I didn't know it must have been a sad song, for somebody!
He was so jaunty, light in his eyes and laugh lines around
them, it was his happy song, happy with me, it was 1942 or 4,
and he was 53.

AN EX-ATHLETE, NOT DYING

to Steve Carey

& so I took the whole trip

filled with breaths, heady with assurance

gained in all innocence from that self's

possession of a sure stride, a strong heart,

quick hands, & what one sport would surely describe

as that easy serenity born of seemingly having been

"a quick read." "He could read the field from before

he even knew what that was." He was so right. Long before.

It was so true. I postulated the whole thing.

It was the innocence of Second Avenue, of one

who only knew about First. I didn't win it;

I didn't buy it; I didn't bird-dog it; but I didn't dog it.

I could always hear it, not see it. But I rarely had

to listen hard to it. I sure didn't have to "bear" it.

I didn't think, "Later for that." I knew *something,*

but I didn't know that. But I didn't know,

brilliant mornings, blind in the rain's rich light,

now able always to find water, that now I would drink.

CODA : SONG

When having something to do
but not yet being at it
because I'm alone, because of you
I lay down the book, & pick up the house

& move it around until it is
where it is what it is I am doing
that is the something I had to do
because I'm no longer alone, because of you.

IN ANSELM HOLLO'S POEMS

The goddess stands in front of her cave.

The beetle wakes up. The frightened camper watches

The two horsemen. The walking catfish walks by.

The twins are fighting the wind let loose in the dark

To be born again the human animal young in the day's events.

The laundry-basket lid is still there.

The moving houses are very moving.

The last empress of China

Is receiving the new members of the orchestra

Through two layers of glass in The Empress Hotel.

In the wreck of the cut-rate shoe store the poet can be seen,

Drunk; a monster; the concussed consciousness in

The charge of the beautiful days. The difficulties are great.

The colors must be incredible: it all coheres:

The force of being she releases in him being

The claim of the dimensions of the world.

POSTCARD FROM THE SKY

You in love with her

read my poems and wonder

what she sees in you.

LAST POEM

Before I began life this time
I took a crash course in Counter-Intelligence
Once here I signed in, see name below, and added
Some words remembered from an earlier time,
"The intention of the organism is to survive."
My earliest, & happiest, memories pre-date WWII,
They involve a glass slipper & a helpless blue rose
In a slender blue single-rose vase: Mine
Was a story without a plot. The days of my years
Folded into one another, an easy fit, in which
I made money & spent it, learned to dance & forgot, gave
Blood, regained my poise, & verbalized myself a place
In Society. 101 St. Mark's Place, apt. 12A, NYC 10009
New York. Friends appeared & disappeared, or wigged out,
Or stayed; inspiring strangers sadly died; everyone
I ever knew aged tremendously, except me. I remained
Somewhere between 2 and 9 years old. But frequent
Reification of my own experiences delivered to me
Several new vocabularies, I loved that almost most of all.
I once had the honor of meeting Beckett & I dug him.
The pills kept me going, until now. Love, & work,
Were my great happinesses, that other people die the source
Of my great, terrible, & inarticulate one grief. In my time
I grew tall & huge of frame, obviously possessed
Of a disconnected head, I had a perfect heart. The end
Came quickly & completely without pain, one quiet night as I
Was sitting, writing, next to you in bed, words chosen randomly
From a tired brain, it, like them, suitable, & fitting.
Let none regret my end who called me friend.

SMALL ROLE FELICITY

for Tom Clark

Anselm is sleeping; Edmund is feverish, &
Chatting; Alice doing the *Times* Crossword Puzzle:
I, having bathed, am pinned, nude, to the bed
Between *Green Hills of Africa* &
The Pro Football Mystique. Steam is hissing
In the pipes, cold air blowing across my legs . . .
Tobacco smoke is rising up my nose, as Significance
Crackles & leaps about inside my nightly no-mind.
Already it's past two, of a night like any other:
O, Old Glory, atop the Empire State, a building, &
Between the Hudson & the East rivers, O, purple, & O, murky black,
If only . . . but O, finally, you, O, Leonardo, you at last arose
Bent, and racked with fit after fit of coughing, & Cursing!
Terrible curses! No Joke! What will happen? Who
be served? Whose call go unanswered? And
Who can 44 down, "Pretender to
The Crown of Georgia?" be . . .
(Boris Pasternak?)

Books by Ted Berrigan

POETRY:

A LILY FOR MY LOVE
THE SONNETS
SEVENTEEN (with Ron Padgett)
LIVING WITH CHRIS (with Joe Brainard)
BEAN SPASMS (with Joe Brainard & Ron Padgett)
MANY HAPPY RETURNS
IN THE EARLY MORNING RAIN
DOUBLE—TALK (with Anselm Hollo)
GUILLAUME APOLLINAIRE IST TOT
MEMORIAL DAY (with Anne Waldman)
A FEELING FOR LEAVING
RED WAGON
NOTHING FOR YOU
TRAIN RIDE
SO GOING AROUND CITIES

PROSE:

CLEAR THE RANGE
BACK IN BOSTON AGAIN (with Tom Clark & Ron Padgett)
YO-YO'S WITH MONEY (with Harris Schiff)

TRANSLATION:

THE DRUNKEN BOAT (with Joe Brainard)

Index of Titles & First Lines

FIRST LINES ARE IN ITALICS

The Selected Works Series